A FORENSIC FORUM

ROBIN ODELL

MANGO
BOOKS

First Edition (Hardcover) 2017
This Edition (Softcover) 2019
Copyright © Robin Odell, 2017, 2019

The right of Robin Odell to be identified as the author
of this work has been asserted in accordance with the
Copyright, Designs & Patents Act 1988.

All rights reserved. No part of this book may be reprinted or reproduced
or utilised in any form or by any electronic, mechanical or other means,
now known or hereafter invented, including photocopying and recording,
or in any information storage or retrieval system, without the prior
permission in writing of the publishers.

All images courtesy Wellcome Library, London

ISBN: 978-1-911273-11-0 (hardcover)
ISBN: 978-1-911273-56-1 (softcover)
ISBN: 978-1-911273-12-7 (ebook)

Published by Mango Books
www.mangobooks.co.uk
18 Soho Square
London W1D 3QL

A
FORENSIC
FORUM

CONTENTS

AUTHOR'S INTRODUCTION 1

PREFACE 3

PART ONE: FORENSIC ESSAYS
Knowing How To Doubt: Forensic Medicine 11
The Realm of Small Things: Forensic Chemistry 23
Biting the Bullet: Forensic Ballistics 35
Your Teeth Cannot Lie: Forensic Odontology...................................... 41
Hatched and Matched: Forensic Entomology 53
Reading the Bones: Forensic Anthropology 63
Pushing up the Daisies: Forensic Botany 69
It's All in the Mind: Forensic Psychiatry 81

PART TWO: BIOGRAPHIES 87

BIBLIOGRAPHY 179

INDEX 183

A Forensic Forum

AUTHOR'S INTRODUCTION

This is the story of forensics told through the lives and discoveries of the great scientific innovators. These thinkers, originators and pioneers, many of whom have been forgotten, shaped the scientific advances that revolutionised the investigation of crime.

We have become accustomed to seeing murder depicted on film and television with forensic investigators be-gloved and clad in protective clothing. This is designed to prevent contamination of the crime scene and *corpus delicti*. Safeguarding the integrity of trace evidence is one of the foundation stones of crime scene investigation, or CSI, as it is known.

Once the province of police surgeons and forensic pathologists, the investigation of crime has expanded to draw in a broad spectrum of supporting disciplines. From small beginnings, some of these have become major sciences. Forensic entomology is an example but who remembers its originator? He was Professor Jean Pierre Mégnin whose research, published in 1894, established a new way of estimating time of death by analysing insect activity on corpses.

Prior to 1900, a criminal suspect with blood on his clothes could claim that it was of animal origin and no one could contradict that assertion. At least not until Dr. Paul Uhlenhuth came up with the precipitin test which made it possible to differentiate human from animal blood. This discovery helped to establish serology as a discipline in its own right with forensic and wider applications.

A FORENSIC FORUM

These innovators and many others are included in this story of forensics which is presented in two parts. The first part consists of short essays focussing on the development of the principal disciplines, while the second features a directory in an A to Z format, comprising a hundred biographies covering a span of five centuries of the principal forensic innovators.

The chief aim of the book is to pay tribute to the legion of scientific pioneers who devoted their skills and ingenuity to the creation of a forensic skills base. While many of them have faded into the mists of time, their achievements live on in the daily implementation of forensic science used to solve crimes worldwide.

ROBIN ODELL
Sonning Common, South Oxfordshire
2017

PREFACE

Since the beginnings of organised human society, death, in all its mystery, has captivated the mind and prompted many questions. For the Greeks, death was considered to be the twin brother of sleep and, for the Romans, it became a political tool. That every death should be explained is a long-standing requirement of organised societies.

Publicly observed deaths, joining cause and effect, became matters of record. Thus, in the 4th century BC, Aeschylus, the Greek poet, was killed by a tortoise which fell from the talons of an eagle flying above and fatally struck him on the head. Unusual cause and deadly effect were recorded as history. Moving forward to the Roman era, publicly witnessed assassination of political figures became a common occurrence. Julius Caesar was one such victim. Assassins took his life in 44BC, having inflicted twenty-three knife wounds on his body.

While these observable events involved accidental death in the case of Aeschylus and assassination in the taking of Caesar's life, there remained the unexplained deaths of ordinary citizens, victims of murder, accident or suicide. The need to understand these events required detailed explanation.

The Romans led the way, seeking to resolve these enquiries by formulating the *lex fori*, or law of the Forum. This was the origin of the term forensic, the application of knowledge to the service of the law – hence, forensic medicine. The practice of dealing with an unexplained or suspicious death was to place the body in the Forum

Romanum so that it could be viewed publicly and conclusions drawn. The idea was to see and explain.

As enquiries into unexplained deaths, possibly as the result of criminal actions, deepened, so investigations became more focussed. What emerged were the simple questions of who, how, what and why? The identities of victim and perpetrator were crucial and it was important to establish the method of killing and the motive. Answers to these questions helped to reconstruct the circumstances of deaths that were outside the domain of natural causes.

Interpretation of injuries was a task that naturally fell to the physicians in the community. While deaths resulting from bludgeoning or knife wounds were fairly obvious, fatalities due to asphyxiation or poisoning were more tricky. A major obstacle which defeated those seeking to provide answers was simply that they knew very little about human anatomy and the structures inside the body.

There were few better places to learn than the battlefields of Europe where military surgeons attended the wounded and dying. One such was a French surgeon, Ambroise **Paré**, who learned how to probe and assess all manner of wounds. In so doing, he laid the foundations of forensic pathology.

A breakthrough in understanding came in 1543 when Andreas **Vesalius** published his studies on the structure of the human body. For the first time, doctors had at their command knowledge of the interior form and workings of the body. This was followed by Morgagni's studies of morbid anatomy related to what he described as the "seats and causes of disease". The stage was set for a leap forward in scientific understanding of the processes which governed life and death.

The next significant development was the microscope which opened up a whole new vista of understanding of the unseen labyrinths of the body. The discovery of blood corpuscles showed that even body fluids had structure as did the hairs on the head. Microscopy made disease accessible and revealed its affect on the tissues. In due course, this led to the development of histology and examination of tissues at cellular level.

The powers afforded by the magnifying lens brought together

two leading crime specialists in an unusual interface between fact and fiction. In the early 1900s, Arthur Conan **Doyle**, famed crime writer, and Edmond **Locard**, a leading French scientist, met to discuss matters of mutual interest. Their chief discussion topic was trace evidence.

Doyle's great detective, Sherlock Holmes, armed with his handheld magnifying glass, was a keen observer of the phenomenon whereby commonplace materials such as soil, vegetation and dust, were picked up and transferred from place to place. Any close contact between two individuals results in a transfer of these materials which are often microscopic in nature. This type of exchange had been noted by Locard and put on a scientific basis, embodied in his famous dictum that every contact leaves a trace.

Thinking along these lines placed a new emphasis on examining a crime suspect's body and clothing and ensuring that a crime scene remained untouched until it could be closely examined by forensic specialists. This principle was taken up by Hans **Gross**, an Austrian magistrate who had also met Conan Doyle. One result was that the concept of evidence transfer was included in an edition of Gross's landmark guide to criminology which established police science as a discipline in its own right. Not surprisingly, the microscope played a significant role in these new developments.

From these firm foundations came recognition that forensic medicine and forensic science needed an academic basis to promote the new thinking. Europe's leading centres of learning responded by setting up professorships and started teaching programmes that would inspire future generations. New forensic applications based on traditional disciplines such as chemistry, botany and entomology began to emerge. One outstanding characteristic became evident among forensic practitioners which was their willingness and desire to share knowledge. These interchanges allowed one idea to spark off another in a different field with far-reaching benefits.

The emphasis in the forensic world kept changing and newly emerging activities, once tagged on to established disciplines, became sciences in their own right. Thus, toxicology, under the guiding hand of Mathieu **Orfila**, once an adjunct of forensic chemistry, became a discipline in its own right. And the same was true of serology. Other, more seismic changes, were also taking place and, as the nineteenth century drew to a close, fingerprinting as a means of identification superceded the system of anthropometry pioneered by Alphonse **Bertillon**.

Another shift of emphasis came early in the twentieth century with developments in the USA, chiefly those in the fields of anthropology and ballistics. That teeth and bones could help to determine identity had become established in Europe with the rise of forensic dentistry which had been drawn into the wider scope of advances made in America in anthropological studies. Examining skeletal remains became the province of the "bone doctors" who used measurements of the long bones as a means of establishing an individual's height.

This concept had been pioneered in France by **Lacassagne** and formulae developed which enabled calculations to be converted into height measurements. "Reading the bones" became a significant discipline enabling anthropologists to reconstruct the likely physical characteristics of long dead individuals. Facial reconstruction techniques were also developed based on the structural elements of skulls.

These developments had far reaching significance both historically and contemporaneously. By combining the potential of odontology and anthropology, the remains of otherwise unidentifiable individuals, obliterated by warfare, genocide, terrorism and natural disasters, such as fire and transportation accidents, could be identified and their individuality restored.

Another major development was that of forensic ballistics which transformed the investigation of gun crime. That every gun leaves characteristic markings on each bullet fired from it had been remarked upon by Victor **Balthazard** in 1913. And, once again, a major forensic development was aided by the power of microscopic enlargement. The invention of the comparison microscope by scientists in the USA was as significant in its field as fingerprints were to identification.

The ability to view bullets side-by-side in an enlarged viewing field opened up an important diagnostic technique based on comparison. In a world seemingly obsessed with firearms and with rising homicide rates, this advance revolutionised police work on firearms examination.

PREFACE

Establishing time of death is one of the tasks regularly faced by forensic pathologists. Estimates based on the condition of a body, including temperature, rigor mortis and lividity are important in deaths that have occurred within forty-eight hours of discovery. Beyond that timing, things become a little more difficult, especially where a body has started to decompose.

Bodies found outdoors are subject to environmental conditions including variations in temperature and humidity, the nature of the ground and attacks by animals and insects. Corpses infested by insects are of special significance, as Jean Pierre **Mégnin** showed in his studies in the late nineteenth century. He demonstrated that knowledge of the life cycle of blowflies could provide accurate indications of the time that had elapsed since death. This was the beginning of forensic entomology and led to techniques based on analysing insect life on a degrading corpse to provide an accurate guide to the post mortem interval.

Estimating time of death lay behind the body farm research carried out in the USA by William **Bass** in the 1980s. He simulated a variety of burial conditions to determine the process of degradation. This included the effect of insect populations on a corpse related to the time which had elapsed since death. This was literally ground-breaking research which demonstrated the value of combining forensic sciences; in this case, entomology and anthropology.

Once investigators have provided answers to the who?, what?, where?, when? and how? of a murder case, that leaves possibly the last forensic hurdle, why? It is a facet of the violent nature of human behaviour that has puzzled observers for centuries. Some of the reasons for killing another human being – gain, jealousy, envy, elimination and revenge – make a kind of sense as understandable emotions. What forensic psychiatrists grapple with are the more obscure triggers which allow these impulses to override accepted moral codes.

Since the late eighteenth century, jurists and psychiatrists have attempted to define guilty intention in ways that distinguish legal insanity from true culpability. Various formulae have been devised encompassing concepts of diminished responsibility, irresistible impulses and recognised mental disorders such as schizophrenia. While, in the public domain, terms such as psychopath and sociopath have been used to explain aberrant behaviour.

It has been acknowledged that emotional and environmental circumstances can affect individual reactions, and developments in neuroscience offer possible reasons. Included in these is the use of modern technology which allows detailed scans to be made of the brain in a search for demonstrable defects that might explain uncontrolled reactions and violent behaviour.

All of this is a far cry from Cesare **Lombroso**'s concept of the born criminal distinguished by his outward appearance and harbouring base instincts like those of an inferior animal. Lombroso noted apelike features in the skulls of known criminals which he viewed as the "seat of the great disturbance". While his theories have long been discredited, his focus on the brain was, possibly, well-founded.

Searching for a "crime gene" does not feature in contemporary psychiatry but there are reasons for believing that emotional and environmental factors affecting human behaviour may be triggered genetically. The search for answers to the question why do individuals kill, continues and neuroscience, aided by ever more sophisticated technology, broadens its enquiries into the innermost reaches of the brain.

The history of forensic science has been to link cause and effect in the context of charting the deep waters of human criminality. This has been achieved through the pioneering creativity of generations of innovators whose willingness to override outmoded concepts and share new information has been exceptional. Scientific disciplines provide a better understanding of crime in all its varied aspects and they are offered in the spirit of serving the cause of justice.

PART ONE :
FORENSIC ESSAYS

KNOWING HOW TO DOUBT

Forensic Medicine

After he fell victim to the knives of assassins in 44BC, the wounds on Julius Caesar's body were examined by Antistius, an established Roman jurist of the time. This was, perhaps, the beginning of forensic medicine, although scholars might dispute it. The Forum Romanum was the place where Romans gathered to discuss public affairs and to consider explanations of sudden deaths. Hence, the origin of the term 'forensics', meaning a "court or a forum". The branch of medical practice interacting with the law became known as forensic medicine and the word 'forensic' entered into English usage in 1659.

Links between medicine and the law first emerged in China in 1248 with the publication of a work that explored ways in which medical knowledge could be used to help solve crimes and process them through the legal system. Another two hundred and fifty years would elapse before forensic medicine emerged in Europe and the application of medical knowledge to legal proceedings inspired the term, medico-legal, which has endured to the present day. Its essence is to use medical procedures and legal logic to explain injuries and suspicious loss of life. French and Italian physicians directed their attentions to the effects of violence inflicted on the human body. By these means, they made it possible to distinguish between murder, accident and suicide.

A FORENSIC FORUM

The first attempt to coordinate medical-legal work was published in 1507 under the authority of the Bishop of Bamberg in Germany. This was a model penal code and, six years later, Henry IV of France issued a decree that every town and city should appoint two surgeons to examine and report on incidents of violence and murder. While this was in the spirit of public accountability pioneered in ancient Rome, a landmark development came in 1543 when Andreas **Vesalius**, a Flemish anatomist, published his study on *The Structure of the Human Body*.

Based on his dissection and examination of human cadavers, the work of Vesalius was to become a cornerstone in the development of medicine as a scientific discipline. He was assisted by a highly-skilled illustrator, Jan Stephen van Calcar, whose drawings graced the pages of the anatomist's seven-volume study. The collaboration of these two innovators resulted in the first accurate knowledge of human anatomy and, in the process, dispelled many of the centuries' old myths which had previously hampered understanding. For the first time, physicians were able to penetrate the deep secrets of human anatomy which had for so long been protected by religious laws prohibiting human dissection.

Emboldened by the revelations of Vesalius who had provided what in modern parlance might be described as a Sat-Nav of the human body, German doctors began to formalise the new knowledge and draw it into their teaching programmes. It was a slow process, with the first lectures on forensic medicine being presented in Leipzig in 1640.

Rapid advances in medical science, embracing pathology and toxicology came into the reckoning and practical manuals and textbooks were published in Germany and France. In particular, a treatise on legal medicine published in France in 1796 started a trend to share the new learning with a wider medical audience.

The French Revolution provided a further impetus and, in 1808, the Napoleonic Code dispensed with the secrecy hitherto shrouding criminal proceedings and paved the way for greater openness. Again, this echoed the spirit of the public medicine practised centuries earlier in the Forum Romanum.

Doctors began to focus on the issues involved in deaths marked by fatal violence such as the identity of victims, the time of death and the nature of injuries inflicted. Critical elements such as rigor mortis, body temperature and lividity came under scrutiny as time markers. Wounds were probed to assess penetration and damage to vital organs together with the more elusive indications of asphyxiation, drowning and poisoning. Post mortem examination became an essential part of the forensic pathologist's discipline.

One of the pioneers of these new approaches was Alexandre **Lacassagne**, a French physician based in Lyon and practising in the late nineteenth century. He made a particular study of the cooling rates of bodies after death and took forensic medicine into new realms. Most importantly, he recognised the uncertainties involved in interpreting post mortem characteristics. He cautioned that "One must know how to doubt", a guiding maxim that would be observed by generations of future pathologists.

It would fall to Lacassagne to make one of the most outstanding breakthroughs in applied forensic medicine. In 1889, he was asked to examine the rotting corpse of a man found in a sack by the riverside at Lyon. What happened next has been comprehensively covered by Jürgen Thorwald in his book, *Dead Men Tell Tales*, published in 1966. But the essential details merit retelling. The rotting remains were thought to be those of Toussaint-Augssent Gouffé, a court bailiff who had gone missing in Paris two months previously. But how to prove identity was the question facing the police.

Looking at the decomposing corpse and skeletal remains, Lacassagne set about measuring the long bones of the legs and arms in an attempt to determine the individual's height. It was known that there was a correlation between the body's long bones and height and formulae existed for making these determinations. By applying this method, the pathologist worked out that the man would have been about five feet eight inches tall. Next, he found that due to a deformity in his right leg, the man would have walked with a limp. These two factors matched what was known about Gouffé but it was still short of confirming identity.

Continuing his examination and searching for a cause of death, Lacassagne found that a cartilage in the throat of the corpse was broken, an indication of strangulation. Next, he looked at the teeth with a view to establishing the individual's age. In an age before forensic dentistry had been conceived, the pathologist determined from the pattern of wear that the man was probably aged about fifty years. As events turned out, this proved to be a remarkable estimate; Gouffé, the missing man, had been aged forty-nine.

By applying and adapting the latest forensic practices, Lacassagne had determined the man's height, age and the fact that he had a limp. All of which pointed to Gouffé. The final test for identity and one which presaged later developments, was to examine the head hair on the corpse, and compare it with a sample retrieved from Gouffé's hairbrush. Using microscopic analysis, he found that the samples matched. He had without doubt confirmed that the dead man was indeed the missing bailiff. In due course, Gouffé's killers were traced and they made a confession to murder and disposing of the victim's body. They had, though, reckoned without Lacassagne and his outstanding forensic skills.

The advent of the twentieth century brought a spate of developments in the science of crime solving, chief among them being fingerprints, blood analysis and trace evidence. The principle that every contact between victim and assailant involved an exchange of trace evidence had long been understood but the lack of methods to exploit it vexed the police.

Blood transferred from an injured victim to his attacker's clothing or weapon was a classic. If a murder suspect was sufficiently astute, he might try to explain the presence of any such stains by claiming they were of animal origin and his claim could not be disproved. At least not until 1901 when Dr. Paul **Uhlenhuth**, a German scientist, developed the precipitin test which enabled human blood to be distinguished from that of an animal source.

In the previous year, Dr. Karl **Landsteiner** had pioneered the science of blood grouping. This was another important development in the science which could be used to establish the possible origin of a human bloodstain. And Lacassagne, never far from the frontiers of investigation, had made a study of blood spots and splashes to work out the position of an assailant relative to his victim. This was the beginning of systematic crime scene investigation, CSI, as it would become known, and the development of a new science, that of blood spatter analysis. In the 1970s, Herbert Leon **MacDonell**, an American criminologist, would make a special study of the physics of blood patterns.

KNOWING HOW TO DOUBT: FORENSIC MEDICINE

Another kind of contact trace often found at a crime scene or during post mortem examination is hair which the victim, in the course of a violent struggle, might tear from the head of an assailant. Such was the case when Dr. Victor **Balthazard** was called out to a crime scene in Paris in 1909.

A woman had been brutally bludgeoned to death, sustaining multiple wounds. Clutched in her hand was a tuft of hair presumed to have been torn from her attacker's head. By carefully measuring the diameter of each hair and evaluating its colour, he believed the assailant was likely to be a woman. The police had two suspects, both female, and by comparing hair samples, Balthazard was able to eliminate one but point the finger at the other who confessed to the murder.

Hair is extremely durable and remains identifiable even on decomposing bodies or when attached to a discarded weapon. By microscopic examination it is possible to tell which part of the body detached hair had originated. Hair is also highly absorbent which is particularly useful in cases of suspected poisoning when, for example, arsenic can be revealed by chemical analysis.

As with blood, it is important to know if trace evidence involving hair comes from a human or an animal source. In 1910, Balthazard published a book, *Hairs of Mammalia*, which set out the various distinguishing characteristics. There is more to hair than meets the eye and, apart from length and colour, individual hairs have structure and, depending on how they have been gleaned, roots. Significantly, microscopic examination of hair can also determine whether it is of human or animal origin.

The knowing how to doubt principle came full circle in 2015 when the value of hair analysis for identification purposes was questioned following several controversial cases in the USA. Microscopic analysis of a single hair was used as evidence of identification and played a major role in obtaining criminal convictions. In consequence, a number of individuals were sentenced to death and executed using what the FBI later admitted was flawed evidence.

The exploitation of single hair microscopic analysis had been given a level of certainty that was not justified and, hence, fell into disrepute. Hair analysis still has a part to play in forensic examination and, used in conjunction with other evidence, to establish identification and eliminate suspects.

The pioneering French criminologist, Dr. Edmond **Locard**, set the agenda for crime scene investigation when he stated that "every contact leaves a trace". Others followed this path, developing ever more sophisticated methods to examine the wealth of materials, natural and man-made, which forensic examiners might encounter in the course of their post mortem work. Every nook and cranny of the human body is a potential depository for contact traces, from the inner recesses of the ear and nose to grime under the fingernails.

Following the pre-eminence of French forensic experts, the focus changed in the 1900s as attention turned to Scotland where a rich heritage was developing. Forensic medicine had been slow in taking root in Britain and, although it emerged as a new discipline around 1788, it would be another decade before the first formal lectures were presented at Edinburgh University. These were delivered in 1801 by Dr. Andrew **Duncan**, the elder and, in honour of his achievements, the first professorship was awarded to his son, known as Andrew Duncan the younger, in 1807.

There followed a tradition of Scottish-based professors of forensic medicine in which son followed father, namely the Littlejohns of Edinburgh and the Glaisters at Glasgow. Another stalwart of forensic medicine in Scotland was Sir Sydney **Smith** who became Regius Professor at Edinburgh. He extended his professional scope by working abroad where he developed pioneering advances in what came to be known as forensic ballistics – the examination of firearms evidence.

If any of these practitioners was qualified to comment on the qualities needed by a forensic examiner, it was surely Smith. He wrote that, "A knowledge of medicine and a stock of common sense are not in themselves sufficient…". He believed that the forensic medical examiner needed a working knowledge of many subjects which had a bearing on death and the conditions to which a body had been exposed. He was a strong advocate of enlisting the involvement of specialists such as chemists, biologists, toxicologists and other practitioners involved in crime solving.

Toxicology, in particular, became a strong ally of forensic medicine not least due to the propensity of poisoners to use their lethal potions and get away with murder. This changed dramatically as chemists established methods of determining the presence of toxic materials both in the living and the dead.

As things evolved, so came the man, in this case, Mathieu **Orfila**, who would be given the accolade of "Father of Toxicology". His treatise on poisons, published in 1813, brought together everything known at that time about poisons and their effects. He remained a pivotal figure in his discipline for forty years and toxicology and forensic medicine remained closely linked. The symbiosis could be measured by the number of pages that toxicology commanded in textbooks. William Guy's book on Forensic Medicine published in 1861 contained over two hundred pages devoted to toxicology.

Building on the example set by Locard, Sydney Smith, fascinated by the interpretation of crime scene evidence, spoke about "the principle of interchange". The concept helped to define the knowledge base needed by coming generations of forensic examiners. One of the most important principles to emerge from this thinking related to the sanctity of the crime scene. The golden rule was to disturb nothing until a systematic examination had been made of the location. It was as important to prevent the introduction of unrelated trace elements as it was not to disturb the scene. Hence, in news coverage of crime investigation, we see detectives and forensic specialists, wearing gloves and protective clothing.

New vistas had also been opened up by the microscope and its use to examine body tissues in close detail. The science of histology emerged and became an important adjunct to forensic medicine. Dr. Hans **Gross** helped to revolutionise police investigative procedures by introducing scientific methods including photography and microscopy. In 1893, he published a book on criminology which set out step-by-step procedures for conducting a criminal investigation. It was the foundation of what came to be called police science. He pointed out that all round alertness at the crime scene was imperative, not least because medical examiners sometimes missed important clues. Gross was a lawyer by profession who knew there was always a time to doubt.

A vital aspect of crime scene examination which began to be implemented at the end of the nineteenth century, was that of recording the physical details. In an age before photography, medical examiners made notes and sketches. An exemplar was Dr. F Gordon Brown who was called to the scene of one of Jack the Ripper's murders in 1888. He made sketches of the injuries inflicted on the victim's body and compiled a comprehensive post-mortem report. This was a discipline that survived well into the next century, even when photography became commonplace. Professor Keith Simpson developed an artistic flair which he used to illustrate crime scene details well into the 1960s.

The discovery of X-rays by Wilhelm Röntgen in 1875 had already been exploited by forensic pathologists, notably in the Ruxton case in 1935. Professors **Glaister** and **Brash** combined radiography and photography to very good effect in identifying the remains of Ruxton's victims.

The baton of forensic medicine had, to a certain extent, been passed on to Great Britain with a succession of celebrated practitioners. The first challenge was to overcome the opprobrium of the "Beastly Science". This was the description of their profession which followed an unfortunate episode in 1859 when Dr. Alfred Swaine **Taylor** gave evidence at the trial of Dr. Smethurst who was accused of poisoning his partner with arsenic. Dr. Taylor claimed to have found what appeared to be incriminating traces of arsenic in a medicine bottle. It was only during the legal process that he realised his test reagents were contaminated by arsenical impurities which invalidated his results. Smethurst was reprieved because of this error and the reputation of forensic medicine was severely dented.

The advance of the twentieth century brought a surge of public interest in the process of medico-legal matters and, in particular, the drama sometimes associated with major murder trials. These were proceedings in which forensic experts demonstrated their specialised knowledge and presented their findings. Newspapers of the day made much of this interest in criminal matters and reported trials in great detail. This process involved directing a spotlight onto forensic pathologists who, not of their own choosing, became public figures as a result. All of which helped dispel the bad feeling that had clung to the "Beastly Science". The public now became enthralled by celebrity pathologists, such as Sir Bernard **Spilsbury** and Sir Sydney Smith.

The USA was slow to take up the advances in forensic medicine being forged in Europe, chiefly due to the coroner system which governed medico-legal work. Coroners were not necessarily medically qualified but elected officials who were supposed to apply common sense to criminal matters. By 1877, the system was regarded as not fit for purpose and changes quickly followed.

One of the problems was the lack of experienced forensic pathologists. This changed in 1917 when Dr. Charles **Norris** was appointed Chief Medical Examiner of New York City. He brought with him a combination of skills as a physician and pathologist, some of which he had learned from time spent working in Germany and Austria. In 1934, he was successful in setting up a department of forensic medicine at New York University. This was a major step forward in the development of forensic skills in America.

It was, perhaps, not surprising, in a nation dedicated to gun ownership, that advances in forensic ballistics should be made in the USA. Alexandre Lacassagne had observed in 1889 that marks found on a bullet might relate to the weapon which fired it. This notion was pursued in the USA by Charles E. **Waite** and Philip **Gravelle** who established the Bureau of Forensic Ballistics in New York in 1923.

A major breakthrough came with Gravelle's invention of the comparison microscope which allowed two bullets to be examined in the same field of vision. Aided by Calvin **Goddard**, a former army doctor, they put forensic ballistics on the map, notably in the Sacco and Vanzetti case in 1927. The comparison microscope showed without doubt that Sacco's handgun had fired the shots which claimed two victims in a robbery. Thus was established the principle that every gun barrel leaves unique marks on the bullets fired from it – a weapon's fingerprint, one might say.

The history of forensic medicine is of a succession of giant leaps forward, including serology, trace evidence, toxicology and ballistics. In 1984 came a truly revolutionary advance with the development of DNA fingerprinting. Dr. Alec **Jeffreys**, a geneticist working at Leicester University, set himself the task of developing a way of mapping human genes.

Techniques already existed for examining the genes present in human cells and their genetic substance, DNA. Jeffreys' objective was to find a way of demonstrating the individuality of these cells.

The prize was his discovery of DNA fingerprinting, a method of establishing the identity of human individuals that was beyond dispute.

DNA fingerprinting quickly evolved into a new, powerful tool enabling forensic examiners to analyse tissues, blood, saliva and semen, all of which had a DNA story to tell. Crime scene investigation took on a new dimension giving the collection and analysis of trace evidence a new stimulus. DNA could also be used to establish the identity of victims of natural and man-made disasters whose bodies had been virtually destroyed. And, most importantly, while DNA fingerprinting could be used to catch criminals, it also served to protect the innocent. DNA information is easily stored on computers and most countries maintain a national database.

Advances in the use of computerisation also brought dividends for the recording and storing of information one of which is the virtopsy or virtual autopsy. The traditional hands-on approach to post mortem examination is set to change with a radical new approach being developed and tested at the Institute of Forensic Medicine in Zurich.

Unlike traditional autopsies which involve invasive techniques such as cutting and probing, virtopsies leave the corpse intact. This is achieved by using computed tomography to create virtual images in an "all seeing" process which can access the furthest recesses of the body without causing damage. Three-dimensional images are created which can be stored, reviewed at any time and shared between experts. The imaging also has the potential to reveal post mortem features that might be missed using traditional methods and record the precise locations of bullets and bone fragments.

Scientists developing virtopsy believe the new technology has the potential to revolutionise criminal investigation as it applies to post mortem examination. Their stated belief is that "perfect murder" will not be possible in the future. The vision is that where DNA fingerprinting superseded blood grouping analysis, so virtopsy will make the traditional autopsy redundant. The days when Professor Keith **Simpson** appeared at a murder trial holding up a skull in a graphic display of the victim's injuries will become just a distant memory.

Throughout its long and distinguished history, forensic medicine and its practitioners have shown a willingness to learn and adapt to new strategies and techniques. This is consistent with the questioning nature of their profession and the need to explain the effects of criminal acts on those who suffer them. Milton **Helpern**, a former Chief Medical Examiner of the City of New York, described forensic pathology as, "strictly a discovery agency. We are not interested in whodunit," he wrote in his memoir, *Autopsy*, "all we want to know is what did it".

Forensic medicine aims at dispelling doubts and reaching for dependable solutions. But even the best of new technology can only speak to the images it produces, while the pathologist is needed to provide interpretation. History has shown that certainty is elusive which brings us back to one of the great forensic pioneers, Alexandre Lacassagne. "One must know how to doubt", was his personal belief and, perhaps, a guiding principle for an entire profession?

A FORENSIC FORUM

THE REALM OF SMALL THINGS

Forensic Chemistry

It is open to debate when forensic science first became of age. But, probably, chemistry provided the lead. Sir Arthur Conan **Doyle**'s famous detective, Sherlock Holmes, is often depicted as a lone figure working late into the night at his workbench. Surrounded by retorts and other glass vessels as well as the trademark Bunsen Burner, he carries out his analytical tests in the furtherance of crime investigation.

Holmes was said to have a profound knowledge of chemistry and to have indulged the subject as a hobby and even as a form of relaxation. Certainly, his creator was credited with stimulating a scientific approach to crime detection, but the real pioneers came before he made his mark.

James **Marsh**, a chemist working at the Royal Arsenal in Woolwich, London, was fascinated by the work of Karl **Scheele**, a Swedish chemist, who had manufactured arsine gas from white arsenic in 1775. With arsenic poisoning in the news because of a recent murder case, Marsh set about devising a method to detect the poison. The result was the Marsh test, which could identify small quantities of arsenic. This was a breakthrough long awaited by toxicologists. Marsh's triumph was published in Edinburgh in 1836 under the modest title, "*The Test for Arsenic*".

The method was soon in use in a famous French poisoning case in 1840 when Marie Lafarge was tried for killing her husband. The distinguished chemist, Professor Mathieu **Orfila**, used the Marsh test and successfully challenged the defence notion that the use of arsenic as a poison could not be proved.

In 1851 came another breakthrough initiated by a poisoning case, this time in Belgium. Hippolyte de Bocarmé was accused of murdering his brother-in-law out of greed. The dead man had marks around his mouth suggesting corrosive poisoning. Internal organs were taken for further examination, a task which fell to Jean Servais **Stas**, a chemist working at Louvain University.

Stas ruled out corrosive poisoning and also arsenic. Suspecting a vegetable poison was the lethal agent, he embarked on a series of exhaustive tests which enabled him to identify the poison as nicotine. His conclusions were dramatically verified when a further search of Bocarmé's chateau revealed the secret apparatus he used to extract nicotine from tobacco.

Stas's method with modifications endured for a hundred years and was used worldwide. He went on to become Professor of Chemistry at Louvain. The success of Marsh and Stas, who were both chemists, posed the question of whether their achievements lay in the realm of chemistry or toxicology. The fact is, they were pioneers in one discipline which served another. This has been a feature of the way in which the forensic sciences have evolved, where different disciplines complement each other with new discoveries.

This sentiment was voiced by Dr. Hans **Gross**, the far-sighted Austrian magistrate who turned his analytical mind to the needs of crime investigation. Inspired by Sherlock Holmes, he envisioned a systematic approach which embraced every scientific discipline. In his great work, *Criminal Investigation*, published in 1893, he included a chapter on "employment of the chemist". He acknowledged the uniqueness of chemistry in its wide range and many points of contact with other disciplines. Every substance and its chemical composition came within the forensic orbit.

Writing in 1945, Alfred **Lucas** offered a definition of forensic chemistry as "chemistry exercised in the service of the law". He was at pains to point out that it should not be confused with forensic medicine. Regarding the scope of forensic chemistry he wrote that it was "very wide and the boundaries are ill defined".

The world of the forensic chemist is the realm of small things; the fragments, particles, debris and dust created by human activities. The potential of this world was opened up in 1912 by Dr. Edmond **Locard** working at the University of Lyon. He was an admirer of both Conan Doyle and Hans Gross and shared their commitment to science.

When Marie Lafelle was found dead in her parents' home, suspicion was directed at the boyfriend, Emile Gourbin, who was known to harbour jealous feelings about the girl. With little evidence to go on, the police investigation seemed to be faltering. At which point, Locard was asked to assist.

Viewing the dead girl in the mortuary he saw the marks of strangulation on her throat and asked the police if he could examine the fingernails of the suspect. Locard took scrapings from beneath Gourbin's nails and examined them under a microscope. He identified a few epithelial cells which he noted were coated with a pink powdery substance. This proved to be pigmented rice starch used as a constituent in cosmetic face powders.

The next step was to secure the cosmetic preparations which the dead girl was in the habit of using as make-up. Among them was face powder which Locard showed exactly matched the fingernail scrapings. The powder was not a mass-produced cosmetic but one which was specially prepared by a chemist in Lyon who confirmed its constituents.

Confronted with this new evidence, Gourbin confessed to killing his girlfriend in a fit of rage. For his part, Locard had demonstrated the forensic powers of chemistry and, in so doing, laid down one of the fundamental principles of crime investigation which is that every contact leaves a trace. Understanding that interaction between a victim and assailant results in a transfer of trace evidence opened up new vistas for forensic science.

As scientific methods began to make an impact in the field of crime investigation, it fell to the medical doctors to implement them. They were, after all, trained to observe, record and interpret and, so, they tended to be the custodians of all things scientific. Apart from examining bodies and the marks upon them, they used their knowledge to test everything from bloodstains to poisons, often with limited resources for analysis and microscopy.

Examination of the physical properties of hair was a task undertaken by the pathologists and some of them approached it with keen interest. One of these was Dr. Victor **Balthazard**, an inventive Parisian forensic practitioner. In 1909, he was called on to assist in a murder enquiry in which a pregnant woman had been found brutally battered to death in her apartment.

When he examined the body, Balthazard's attention was captured by the clump of hair clutched in one of her hands. She had apparently torn this from her attacker's head in her struggle. The doctor examined it under a microscope and recorded its colour and diameter which matched that of one of the suspects. Significantly, he discovered that some of the hair had roots attached and when he examined the head of the suspect, found a patch of scalp which bore the marks of hair snatched from its roots.

A confession resulted and a conviction for murder followed on the basis of the hair evidence. The next year, Balthazard published his study on human and animal hair which, for more than a decade, was the chief forensic guide to hair examination.

Another pathologist fascinated by the evidential powers of hair was Professor John **Glaister**, based in Glasgow. He published an illustrated guide to human and animal hair in 1931 which was acknowledged as the most comprehensive work available for the purposes of identification and classification.

With the rapid advance of science, came more sophisticated methods requiring laboratory facilities and specialised equipment. This was the point at which forensic science began to emerge in its own right with its own brand of specialists. New discoveries and developments providing more comprehensive and accurate methods came thick and fast. At the forefront were the chemists with a wide remit to detect and analyse.

An area calling for their special skills was the detailed chemical analysis of hair samples. One of the characteristics of hair is that it absorbs elements from the environment in small quantities. This helps in cases of poisoning where, for example, arsenic may be detected in the hair and provide a calendar of the duration of poisoning.

Hair grows at a rate of about 0.44mm a day and the distance between the root of the hair and the appearance of traces of arsenic in its length enables the analyst to determine the onset of poisoning. This was illustrated in 1949 when Margery Radford died in a nursing home after eating food contaminated with arsenic.

Scotland Yard's analyst at the time determined that the dead woman's hair had absorbed arsenic at its roots and which extended 5 centimetres out over a period of 100 to 120 days, or about three months. Suspicion fell on her husband whose guilt was confirmed by other supporting evidence. He took his own life before charges could be brought, but the correctness of the evidence of poisoning was never in doubt.

Once arsenic is absorbed by the hair, it remains there forever. This is a characteristic which has been exploited in some highly controversial attempts to rewrite history by calling on the skills of forensic chemists. A thesis was put forward in 1982 suggesting that Napoleon, who died in exile on the island of St. Helena, had been poisoned with arsenic.

Samples of the former emperor's hair were retrieved from various sources and tested for the presence of arsenic a hundred and sixty years after his death. To the satisfaction of those claiming he was murdered, the results proved positive.

A similar exercise carried out in 1991 on a former US president came to a different conclusion. An attempt was made to show that Zachary Taylor, Twelfth President of the United States, who died in 1850, had been poisoned. The contention was that he had eaten strawberries doctored with arsenic and died, ostensibly, from gastroenteritis.

Those who believed he had been murdered because of his opposition to the spread of slavery campaigned for his body to be exhumed. So, a hundred and forty-one years after he died, Zachary Taylor was exhumed and hair samples tested for the presence of arsenic. To the disappointment of the campaigners, the tests proved negative.

Testing for arsenic has proved controversial and never more so than in the case of Dr. Thomas Smethurst, who in 1859 was tried for poisoning his bigamous wife. The main evidence lay in the presence of arsenic in the dead woman's tissues and also in a medicine bottle which had been discovered as the result of tests carried out by Dr. Alfred Swaine **Taylor**, the government analyst. Smethurst was convicted on the strength of this evidence and sentenced to death.

But, at the last minute, Dr. Taylor admitted in court that his tests were invalid due to impurities which he had since found in the chemical reagents he had used. As a result, Smethurst was pardoned and the role of the expert came under fierce criticism. Taylor had put his reputation at risk by his admission, but his honesty was surely commendable. The incident also underlined the absolute necessity to maintain the integrity of evidence samples by keeping them free of contamination. This became one of the great precepts in the practice of all the forensic sciences and evidence gathering procedures.

An insight into the formidable scope of the forensic chemist's task was provided by Dr. Hamish **Walls** in his book, *Forensic Science*, published in 1974. In a chapter headed, *The Chemist's Problems*, he listed some of the substances encountered, which included adhesives, dyes, inks, metals, oils, plastics, rubber, drugs, hair, fibres and blood.

The examination of suspect bloodstains certainly taxed the chemist's ingenuity. While blood visible on the injuries of a murder victim might be fairly assessed as such, stains on clothing and furnishings, though they might have the appearance of blood, could be something else. Blood on the carpet might not necessarily be what it seemed.

Two questions formed in the minds of early investigators; was the stain actually blood and was it human or animal? Until the dawn of the twentieth century it was not possible to answer either of these questions with certainty. The first attempts to differentiate between human and animal blood were based on microscopic examination of the shapes and numbers of red corpuscles in the sample.

There were also simple chemical tests which gave presumptive results for blood but lacked certainty. For example, a stain treated with hydrogen peroxide would produce a frothing reaction if it was blood. But, then, a number of other substances produced a similar reaction. Further chemical tests evolved which gave indicative results for blood but still lacked certainty.

Until 1901, it was simply not possible to distinguish human from animal blood. Any criminal fleeing a crime scene with what appeared to be blood on his clothes could say, without fear of contradiction, that it was from an animal. But, in that year, a German chemist made a significant breakthrough. Dr. Paul **Uhlenhuth** had been studying ways in which the body adapted its blood supply as a defence against disease.

His experiments included injecting protein from chicken eggs into rabbits. From the animal's blood, he extracted a serum which separated out the protein in the form of a precipitate. Applying this principle more widely, he found that it was possible to distinguish between human and animal blood. The precipitin test, as it was known, revolutionised the analysis of bloodstains and gave investigators the tool they had sought for so long. That the test could be used effectively on old, dried-out stains was an added bonus.

The first time the precipitin test was used in Britain, the results were hedged round with caution. In 1910, two men were put on trial, charged with murdering the owner of a mansion called Gorse Hall in Yorkshire. Both were acquitted for lack of evidence. But there had been strong suspicions against one of them who had been found to have what appeared to be bloodstains on his clothing.

Dr. William **Willcox**, the Home Office Analyst, examined the stains and applied the new precipitin test. The result proved positive for human blood, but in his testimony, Willcox cautiously declined to go beyond confirming that it was of mammalian origin. This left sufficient doubt to secure an acquittal.

Some historians regard Uhlenhuth's work as the beginnings of forensic serology and acknowledged German ascendancy in pioneering new advances. The next breakthrough was Dr. Paul **Landsteiner**'s discovery that every human individual's blood falls into one of four unalterable types. The ABO blood-grouping system is based on the function of the red blood corpuscles and the presence in them of agglutinogen.

By determining the blood group of a crime victim, forensic investigators were able to seek a match with stains found on a suspect's clothing, thereby narrowing their criteria. While matching characteristics were not proof of identity, blood grouping helped to focus enquiries and eliminate innocent parties from further investigation.

Thus, in the space of a few months, forensic researchers had made it possible to identify human blood with certainty and place it in clearly defined groups. These discoveries provided the basis for further refinements, creating sub-categories which narrowed the identification process still further. The human bloodstain thereby came to be ranked in importance with fingerprints.

This still left the forensic chemist with many other stains of unknown origin to be analysed as part of crime scene investigation. With the development of ever more powerful laboratory tools and methods, no suspect stain, particle or fragment escaped the rigours of examination.

Using analytical methods requiring glassware and reagents, à la Sherlock Holmes, chemists carried out qualitative tests to find out what was present and quantitative tests to determine how much. The gradual introduction of new methods of separation and measurement enabled analyses to be carried out quickly and to more exacting standards. In due course, the evolution of instrumentation and the computer management of data would take analysis into undreamt of realms.

Examination of documents was a natural domain for the chemist with its requirement to assess different types of paper and to identify the inks used on them. Analysis of handwriting and typewriting would also be drawn into their net in the pursuit of forgery and fraudulent activities.

One of the earliest cases in which scientific evidence involving writing ink used on a document was tested in court was the trial for murder of Richard Brinkley in 1907. He cultivated a friendship with an elderly lady, Mrs. Blume, who owned a house in London which he coveted. Brinkley drew up a Will which made him the sole beneficiary of her estate. He then fooled Mrs. Blume into signing the document while concealing its true nature and similarly deceived two acquaintances into signing it as witnesses.

Mrs. Blume died within months of the Will being made and Brinkley made a claim on her assets. This move was contested by a relative who took legal action requiring him to prove the validity of the document. Brinkley realised that the two witnesses would be questioned, so he decided to eliminate them. His ruse was to visit one of them, Reginald Parker, who lived in lodgings, on the pretext of buying a dog from him. He placed a bottle of stout on the table while the two of them went outside to look at the dog.

During that brief interlude, the owner of the house turned up with his wife and daughter. They spotted the bottle of stout and decided to sample it. This was a fatal mistake, as the stout intended for Parker had been laced with prussic acid. In consequence, the owner and his wife died of poisoning and their daughter was taken ill. The doctor attending the scene quickly identified prussic acid as the fatal agent and sent the dregs in the stout bottle for analysis.

Following enquiries confirming the fatal poisonings, Brinkley was arrested and his machinations were soon uncovered. The police retrieved a bottle of ink from Parker's lodgings and asked Dr. C. Ainsworth **Mitchell**, a noted analyst, to look at it. The ink in question was a distinctive blue/black product which he tested optically using a tintometer to measure and record the colour intensity. Applying the same method to the ink used on the Will, he found it matched perfectly. He also determined that Mrs. Blume's presumed signature on the Will did not correspond with her usual signature. The matching inks and the discovery of Brinkley's source of prussic acid were sufficient to send him to the gallows.

The skills of the forensic chemist are frequently called on in cases of suspected forgery. Such was the situation in 1983 when Hitler's Diaries became a publishing sensation. Following publication in Germany, in *Stern* magazine, the contents of the sixty handwritten notebooks, allegedly penned by Hitler, were offered for sale around the world.

In the UK, *The Sunday Times* called for tests to be carried out to verify the authenticity of the documents. Initial comparison of the handwriting with that of Hitler tended to confirm they were genuine. But chemical tests on the paper and ink told a different story. The paper on which the documents were written contained constituents that only became available in the early 1950s.

Spectrophotometric analysis of the ink also showed the presence of constituents that were not known to manufacturers in the 1940s.

Enquiries led to a German forger who had made an art out of imitating Adolf Hitler's handwriting. The forger was convicted and given a four-year prison sentence.

The invention of gunpowder and its many explosive variants provided ample scope for the varied talents of forensic chemists. There was increased use of firearms in the pursuit of criminal activities after World War Two. Matching of bullets and cartridges to the weapon which fired them became part of the chemist's portfolio but would quickly inspire a new science, that of forensic ballistics.

The examination of propellants and powder residues, though, was very much in the chemist's domain. The range of chemical propellants, from simple gunpowder to more sophisticated compounds, created investigative opportunities in the field of gun crime. Powder residues left after firing a handgun could help determine the type of projectile fired as could powder grains found on wounds. It was also possible to calculate the distance at which a weapon had been discharged and so build-up a reconstruction of the crime.

Whether or not a suspect had fired a handgun could also be shown by examining his hands. The dermal nitrate test developed in the early 1900s was based on the knowledge that when a weapon was fired, gases were emitted which spread a plume of unburnt powder particles, some of which settled on the hand which pulled the trigger.

Early dermal nitrate tests involved putting a coating of paraffin wax over the hand which lifted off any embedded powder residues. The wax could then be tested for the presence of nitrates, using chemical reagents. The dermal nitrate test was not wholly reliable, as nitrates from innocent sources, such as garden fertilizer, would also give a positive result. Further tests were developed which gave results with other compounds used in propellants as ammunition manufacture became more sophisticated.

While the examination of firearms evidence evolved into the separate science of forensic ballistics, investigation of explosives remained the preserve of the chemist. A textbook example of forensic experts working closely with police investigators occurred in Canada in 1949 in the aftermath of an air disaster.

THE REALM OF SMALL THINGS: FORENSIC CHEMISTRY

A Quebec Airways DC-3 on an internal flight exploded in mid-air on 9 September, killing everyone on board. Airline investigators ruled out any malfunction of on-board systems and concentrated on the baggage compartment which was the seat of the explosion. They quickly came to the view that what they were investigating was not an accident but a criminal act.

Police enquiries established that baggage handlers at Quebec had been given a 28lb package to be put on the flight to St. Baie Comeau. The names of the addressee and the sender had been recorded at the time but detectives found that neither person existed. A freight loader gave a description of the woman who had handed over the package. She was traced and found to have a connection to Albert Guay, whose wife had died in the explosion.

While the police were narrowing their lines of enquiry, the forensic specialists were working on a minute examination of the wreckage in the luggage compartment of the aircraft. The discovery of fragments of copper embedded in destroyed baggage proved to be parts of a blasting cap of a type used in the mining industry. This enabled enquiries to become more focussed.

Meanwhile the police investigation centred on Albert Guay, a watchmaker and jeweller, whose companion had arranged for the package to be shipped as air freight. It was also the case that Guay stood to gain substantially from his wife's life insurance.

Led by Franchère Pépin, a chemist and head of the Institute of Legal Medicine and Police Science at Montreal, scientists carried out extensive chemical tests on what proved to be fragments of the bomb. They identified the explosive as D-1 dynamite, a finding which neatly dovetailed with a detective's discovery that Guay had made enquiries about obtaining supplies of dynamite, ostensibly for destroying tree stumps.

The clincher came when chemists examined materials found in the home of a watchmaker who worked with Guay. Généreux Ruest had been carrying out experiments with copper blasting caps and been unwise enough to leave traces which chemists found matched the copper fragments identified in the aircraft wreckage.

Albert Guay confessed to his crime and, together with his two accomplices, paid the ultimate price. The investigation had proved to be a triumph for Canadian science and police work.

Forensic chemistry provided a springboard for other emerging sciences, including serology, ballistics, document examination and toxicology. The chemists, though, remained masters of the small things – the fragments, stains and traces indicative of criminal activity so vital to crime scene investigation, and which so beguiled Sherlock Holmes.

BITING THE BULLET

Forensic Ballistics

In 1889, Alexandre **Lacassagne**, a professor at the University of Lyon in France, examined a bullet removed from the body of the victim of a fatal shooting. What caught his eye were the marks on the projectile in a pattern of grooves. He wondered if these marks had been made by the barrel of the weapon which fired the bullet. When he examined the revolver retrieved from the murder suspect's apartment, he found seven grooves in the rifling of its barrel which matched the grooves on the lethal bullet. By this means was the murderer identified, and the seed of forensic ballistics planted.

Thus began a new phase in the history of crime detection. Strictly speaking, "ballistics" applied to the projectiles fired by weapons, whereas the new science was based on the relationship between the weapon and the bullets fired from it. Firearms evidence might have been a more comprehensive title, but the term, forensic ballistics, introduced in the 1920s has endured.

Following Lacassagne's lead, there was a steady progression of findings all heading in the same direction. In 1898, Paul **Jeserich**, working in Berlin, took microphotographs of a bullet fired from a suspected murder weapon and compared them with similar images taken of the murder bullet. He noted markings on their otherwise smooth surfaces and observed the same abnormalities on both projectiles.

The next discovery was made in Leipzig in 1905 by Richard

Kockel who hit on the idea of making impressions of crime bullets by rolling them on waxed paper. Using the same method on test-fired bullets, he was able to compare the markings on them. If they corresponded, it followed that the bullets had been discharged from the same weapon.

Then, in 1913, Victor **Balthazard** in Paris, took the comparison rationale a stage further when he noted that the firing pin of every weapon leaves a characteristic mark on the base of cartridges. He also noted that any defects or markings on the breechblock would be transferred to the base of cartridge cases. This occurs when the force of the explosive discharge following the trigger pull slams the base of the cartridge into the breechblock. Transfer of any marks or defects takes place at this time. Balthazard wrote up his findings in a technical paper establishing the principle that markings transferred to cartridges were characteristic of a particular weapon and should be included as part of a ballistics appraisal.

These findings in European centres of research were well received in the USA where the next leap forward in forensic ballistics would be made. Charles E. **Waite**, who worked in the New York State Prosecutor's office, had a passion for collecting information on all types of guns. He recorded details of weapons manufactured in the USA and elsewhere from the 1850s onwards. His aim was to build up a reference collection of firearms.

When Waite met Philip **Gravelle**, whose hobbies included photography and working with a microscope, he found a kindred spirit. They were joined by John H. Fisher who also shared an interest in weaponry. Together, they formed the Bureau of Forensic Ballistics, the first organisation of its kind in the world and, separately, each made ground-breaking developments.

Waite set up an unparalleled collection of data on firearms, Fisher devised an instrument known as a helixometer which made it possible to examine the interior of a gun barrel, and Gravelle constructed a comparison microscope which allowed two bullets to be viewed in the same field of vision. When this trio was joined by Colonel Calvin **Goddard**, an army doctor with an interest in firearms, they became a commanding force in the fast developing world of forensic ballistics.

All this ingenuity was soon put to the test in what became a sensational murder case. In 1920, a payroll robbery in Braintree, Massachusetts, resulted in two deaths by shooting. In the aftermath, two Italian anarchists, Nicola Sacco and Bartolomeo Vanzetti, achieved notoriety throughout America in the follow up to their arrest on murder charges.

When the pair were put on trial, ballistics evidence was given by experts of doubtful integrity. The two defendants were found guilty against a background of prejudice and sentenced to death. The public mood then changed and widespread concern was voiced over the verdict. Following various appeals, an inquiry was launched in 1927 and Calvin Goddard was one of those whose expertise was called on. Using the newly invented comparison microscope he confirmed that the fatal bullets had been fired from Sacco's .32 Colt automatic. The condemned men were executed in 1927.

While the Sacco and Vanzetti case was stuck in limbo, what was described as one of America's "wrong man" murder cases, occurred. In 1924, Father Hubert Dahma, a popular preacher at St. Joseph's Episcopal Church in Bridgeport, Connecticut, was shot dead in front of witnesses. The gunman made his getaway as shocked worshippers looked on. A great public outcry followed and pressure was put on the police to locate the murdering gunman. They quickly rounded up twenty-three year old Harold Israel, described as an itinerant, who was found to be carrying a revolver of the same calibre as the one used to kill Father Dahma. He was identified by witnesses to the shooting and, following intense questioning, made a confession. A police ballistics officer confirmed that the gun found in Israel's possession was the murder weapon.

At his trial, Israel pleaded guilty by reason of insanity and the citizens of Bridgeport awaited the formal delivery of a guilty verdict in court. They had, though, reckoned without the intervention of Homer S. Cummings who was appointed as trial prosecutor. He had strong reservations about the quality of some of the evidence, which included inconsistencies in what witnesses claimed to have seen and, in particular, the validity of the ballistics report. Cummings consulted other ballistics experts whose findings were that the bullet recovered from the victim's body had not been fired from Israel's revolver.

When the trial opened, Cummings stated quite plainly that the case against Israel did not hold up. Then, in an incident worthy of TV sleuth Perry Mason, he loaded the supposed murder weapon and pulled the trigger. To the astonishment of those present, the revolver did not fire. The explanation was simple. Due to a defective firing pin, it could not discharge the bullets. In consequence, Harold Israel was judged to be not guilty and left the court a free man.

The shooting in Connecticut heralded the rise of the firearms expert in the USA and emphasised the importance of proper experience and qualifications. Homer Cummings, a seeker after truth, was appointed Attorney General of the United States in 1933.

A book published two years after Cummings' courtroom triumph set out the criteria for evidence given by competent ballistics experts. The authors of *The Identification of Firearms* J.D. and C.O. Gunther, emphasised the examination of observable marks on crime bullets and cartridges which could be compared with test-fired bullets. They wrote, "Here was an issue based on scientific principles, independent of the unreliability of eyewitnesses with their faulty recollections and doubtful credibilities".

News of the potential for advanced techniques, aided by the invention of the comparison microscope, which used science rather than intuition to solve crimes, travelled quickly. An early convert was Dr. Sydney **Smith** who was medico-legal expert at the ministry of Justice in Cairo. In 1924, he was called on to advise in the investigation of the fatal shooting of Sir Lee Stack in the Egyptian capital city.

Smith built his own comparison microscope and used it to examine some of the bullets fired in the fatal shooting. He established from marks on some of them that they had been modified by turning them into dum-dum bullets to increase their destructive capability. He followed this up with a search of a house occupied by one of the suspects. He found there two engineer's bench vices which had recently been used. Metallic particles adhering to the vices matched filings taken from the crime bullets. As a result, the murderous conspirators were brought to justice in what was acknowledged to be a resounding success for forensic science.

The news from Egypt was widely reported back in Britain and impressed Robert **Churchill**, the firearms examiner, to the extent that he made a visit to the USA to learn at first hand from Calvin

Goddard. Such was the reputation of forensic ballistics in America at this time that J. Edgar Hoover, Director of the FBI, set up a special department in Washington to focus on the developing science. With echoes of Lacassagne's observations made at the end of the previous century, Calvin Goddard wrote in 1926 that the individuality of a gun barrel would leave "the fingerprint of that particular barrel" on every bullet fired from it. Having learned the essentials of the new craft from the master, Robert Churchill was inspired to construct a comparison microscope on his return from the USA.

On both sides of the Atlantic, the proving ground for developments in forensic ballistics lay in the realm of real crimes, usually fatal shootings. Churchill's big moment came in 1927 with the killing of a policeman in an English country lane. PC George Gutteridge was waylaid by his killers and shot twice in the head and, adding a brutal finish to their crime, they shot him in both eyes.

Four months after the murder, two men were arrested and charged. In the course of their getaway, Frederick Guy Browne and William Henry Kennedy stole a car which, when it was found abandoned and searched, revealed a discarded cartridge case. This proved to be from an RLIV bullet of a type manufactured at Woolwich Arsenal in London. The base of the cartridge showed a depression probably caused by the breech of the weapon from which it was fired. Significantly, an RLIV bullet had been extracted from Gutteridge's head wound.

When Browne and Kennedy were rounded up, they were found to be in possession of a loaded Webley revolver which showed a flaw in its breechblock. Robert Churchill now employed his newly acquired skills to examine the firearms evidence. In the course of this, he tested fifty Webley revolvers but did not find in any of them a breech defect which matched that of the suspected murder weapon. Churchill gave compelling evidence at the trial which led to the conviction of the two accused men. In his biography of Churchill, Macdonald Hastings wrote, "The firearms evidence against Browne and Kennedy was tested past all possibility of flaw".

Not surprisingly, the evolution of forensic ballistics put a new emphasis on the interpretation of gunshot wounds by medical examiners. New protocols were called for, together with special knowledge on the part of forensic pathologists. Dealing with a fatal shooting, the examiner is confronted with a long list of questions. Was the shooting the result of accident, suicide or murder? Is the particular injury an entry or exit wound? What type of gun was used? What was the angle and direction of fire? These are answered from two standpoints. The first is the location where the victim was found and, secondly, the post mortem room.

Attention is directed to the position of entry and exit wounds and the interpretation used to determine if the shooting was self-inflicted or an act or murder. In the case of suicide, experience tells the pathologist that there are a number of favoured locations within arm's reach including the side of the head, mouth, forehead and heart region. Such injuries are often contact wounds where the gun muzzle is pressed up to the flesh, leaving characteristic traces. In conventional suicides, the weapon will be found at the scene.

Fatal wounds inflicted at a distance will, typically, cause an entry wound and exit wound on the victim's body, each of which has particular characteristics. By examining the passage of a bullet in a through-and-through wound, the pathologist will seek to establish the angle and direction of fire. Investigation of the scene of shooting may turn up spent cartridges and trace evidence linking the perpetrator to the scene.

Once the body has been removed to the autopsy room, the medical examiner will carry out procedures to determine the course of bullets after they have entered the body. Bullet tracks can be determined by factors such as striking a bone which diverts the projectile inside the body leaving no exit wound. X-ray examination is carried out to ascertain the location of any diverted bullet and retrieve it for scrutiny.

A simplistic way of looking at forensic ballistics is a bringing together of cause and effect. Ballistics being the science of mapping causes while pathology is the process of interpreting the destructive effects of gunshot wounds. Like much in the history of forensic science, gains are achieved by the willingness of different disciplines to work together.

What has been firmly established is the absolute necessity of preserving the integrity of crime scenes, especially weapons and bullet recovery. Fortunately, the days of the ill-trained detective, featured in numerous crime-based films, digging out spent bullets embedded in a wall or door with a penknife, are long gone!

YOUR TEETH CANNOT LIE

Forensic Odontology

It has become fashionable to refer to pioneers in various fields as "Father" of this or that discipline. If forensic dentistry has such a "Father", it is probably Dr. Nathan Keep, who practised in Boston, USA in the mid 1800s.

In the cloistered environment of the Massachusetts Medical College in Boston, two academics quarrelled over an unpaid debt. On 23 November 1849, Dr. George Parkman was reported missing. It was known that he had visited Professor John White Webster who owed him money and now attracted suspicion over his colleague's disappearance. A search of the professor's laboratory turned up body parts which had been incinerated in an assay oven.

The remains included a set of dentures which survived the heat. An inquest concluded that the remains were indeed those of Dr. Parkman and confirmation of identity came from his teeth. His dentist, Dr. Nathan Keep, testified that he had made a denture for Parkman who had a uniquely deformed jaw. The dentist's model of his patient's mouth matched in every detail the denture which had been found in the oven.

Following his conviction for murder, Webster confessed to killing Parkman after an angry exchange of words about his outstanding debt. Such was the publicity associated with this case that 60,000 people visited Boston in the hope of seeing the condemned man before he went to the scaffold.

On 4 May 1897, the sky over Paris was illuminated by a fire at the Bazar de la Charité Ball. This fundraising event for the poor of the city was held in a large wooden building in the 8th Arrondissement which went up in flames, killing one hundred and twenty-six people.

In the aftermath of the blaze, the problem arose of identifying the victims, many of whom had been burnt beyond recognition. To assist in this process, Dr. Oscar **Amoëdo**, professor at the Paris Dental School, was called to the scene. During a lengthy investigation, he and his team, successfully identified all but thirty of the fire victims by examining their teeth. Of course, Cuban born Oscar Amöedo did not suddenly discover that human individuals can be identified by means of their teeth. That had been known since Roman times. But what he established was a systematic way of looking at dental evidence as an adjunct to forensic medicine.

In the year following the fire tragedy in Paris, he published his treatise, *L'Art Dentaire en Médecine Légale*. This was an influential text which put forensic dentistry onto a sound scientific footing. He demonstrated that teeth are remarkably durable and can withstand the passage of time as well as the destructive forces of decomposition and burning. Next to fingerprints and DNA, teeth have proved to be reliable indicators of identity, encompassing age, sex and ethnic origins.

It is perhaps worth mentioning at this point a piece of fiction with a Holmesian touch which served to highlight the importance of forensic dentistry. The fictional medico-legal expert, Dr. John Thorndyke, was the creation of R. Austin Freeman, who was described at the time as a rival to Sherlock Holmes. Freeman had a medical training and took a special interest in scientific developments that had forensic possibilities. Thus, in his story, *The Eye of Osiris*, published in 1911, he shows the pivotal part played by dentistry, aided by X-rays, in helping to identify an otherwise unnamed corpse. He praised the contribution made by dentists in forensic investigation and, all this, at least a decade before the new science became established in Britain.

By the time of Amoëdo's death in 1945, the baton had passed to scientists in Norway where the new science was pursued with enthusiasm and vigour. They established the first organisation to put odontological methods on a systematic basis to assist the police with identification in forensic cases. This was the beginning of Scandinavian pre-eminence in this new field which would continue over the next decade.

An early opportunity to put forensic dentistry on the map in Britain came in 1942 and fell to Dr. Keith **Simpson**, a young pathologist working at Guy's Hospital in London. He was called out to examine a body found in a cellar in South London. A workman involved in demolishing a bomb-damaged church in Vauxhall, unearthed a skeleton which was presumed to be the remains of a victim of the German Blitz.

From the presence of a uterus in the dried-up tissues, Simpson determined that the body was female. Considering the depth at which the skeleton had been found, he doubted that he was dealing with a victim of bombing. He judged that death had occurred twelve to eighteen months before it was discovered, whereas the church had been destroyed two years previously in 1940.

The pathologist's mind turned to the possibility of murder, especially when he found that the body had been dismembered. There was also evidence that an attempt had been made to prevent the body being identified by removing the hands and disfiguring the head. Crucially, though, while the lower jaw was missing, the upper jaw was intact. Examining this relic, Simpson saw possibilities. He commented to the detective leading the investigation, "If you trace her dentist … you'll identify her".

Trawling through reports of missing persons, detectives began to focus on Rachel Dobkin, whose disappearance fifteen months previously had been reported to the police by her sister. Mrs Dobkin's age and height corresponded with calculations made by the pathologist on the skeletal remains. A photograph of the missing woman was provided by her sister who also knew the name of her dentist.

The lady's dental practitioner was Barnet Kopkin whose surgery was in Crouch End. He immediately recognised Rachel Dobkin from the photograph and confirmed that she had been his patient for six years. Referring to his records, he drew a diagram of the teeth in the woman's upper jaw relating to the time he had last treated her. With meticulous care, he impressed the detectives by carefully signing and dating his diagram.

Kopkin later met Simpson at Guy's Hospital and the pathologist conducted him to his laboratory where Mrs Dobkin's skull rested on a bench. As soon as he saw it, the dentist said, "That's my patient … That's Mrs Dobkin. Those are my fillings". The drama reached a peak when Kopkin's diagram was compared with the lower jaw and it was evident there was a perfect match. Keith Simpson recorded the occasion in his memoirs and described the excitement of the moment with satisfaction.

The dentist's detailed records showed all the fillings and gaps in the dentition and included fragments of roots left by extractions which had not appeared on Simpson's X-ray photographs. Further X-rays were taken of the jaw by Sir William Kelsey Fry, senior dentist at Guy's, and he confirmed the position of the root fragments. But, while confirmation of identity was a triumph for the combined efforts of pathologist and dentist, there was little evidence at this stage to show that Rachel Dobkin had been murdered.

Keith Simpson had been curious about some yellow powdery deposits found on the remains which turned out to be slaked lime. He knew that while quicklime had a reputation for destroying flesh, in its slaked form it had the opposite effect and acted as a preservative. Turning to the structures of the throat, he found that the thyroid cartilage was broken and attached to it was a small blood clot, clear evidence of an injury caused before death. This discovery pointed at strangulation.

Suspicion focussed on the dead woman's husband, Harry Dobkin, who, it turned out, was separated from his wife and had failed to comply with a maintenance order. For her part, she had repeatedly pestered him for payment but to no avail. He was tried for murder at the Old Bailey and found guilty. But for the chance hit of a German bomb on the church where he had buried the body and some brilliant detective work by Kopkin and Simpson, he would have got away with murder.

In the post war years, examination of dental evidence in murder cases was still very much the province of the forensic pathologist. When a dental practitioner was involved in the investigation, his role was more or less limited to providing dental records for comparison purposes. But, by the early 1950s, dental expertise was beginning to come into its own with the realisation that it had something unique to contribute.

In the infamous Christie murder case in 1953, when several bodies were found in a house in Notting Hill, the pathologist, Francis **Camps**, was astute enough to recognise some unusual dental work in the jaw of one of the skulls. This was a silver alloy dental crown which a British dentist recognised as an example of Austrian technique. This piece of information enabled investigators to match one of the bodies to an Austrian woman who had been reported missing in 1943.

An early example of a bite mark being used as evidence in a criminological investigation occurred in a burglary case in the North of England in 1906. An intruder took a bite out of a piece of cheese leaving evidence of identity strong enough to convict him. The first identification in Britain of a murderer by bite marks inflicted on his victim, fell to Keith Simpson. On New Year's Day 1948, a young woman's body was found in Tunbridge Wells. She had been beaten and strangled. At post mortem, Simpson found a bite mark on her right breast. He noticed at once the irregular spacing of impressions made by two upper and four lower teeth. He told detectives that he believed he could identify the murderer by his teeth.

It was known that the dead woman had quarrelled with her husband and suspicion focussed on him. He was persuaded to let the pathologist take wax impressions of his teeth which were so irregularly spaced and angled as to simplify comparison with the bite marks left on the body. Keith Simpson found a perfect match and the husband was duly charged and later tried for murder.

Cheese featured in a burglary which took place in Texas in 1954. A piece of cheese found at the crime scene had been bitten into which led investigators to ask the chief suspect to take a bite out of a sample piece of cheese. The result brought together a dentist and a firearms expert who independently came to the same conclusion – that the two sets of bite marks were a match. The burglar was duly convicted and forensic dentistry made unlikely headlines in the Texas newspapers.

Those were pioneering days for a new science and brought

together an interesting combination of expertise. The firearm examiner's knowledge of matching bullets to the weapons that fired them was not too dissimilar to the principle of the dentist matching a set of teeth to a bite mark.

A change in professional emphasis came in 1967 when Dr. Warren Harvey of the Glasgow Dental School sought the help of a pathologist in an investigation involving the murder of a fifteen-year-old girl at Biggar in Lanarkshire. Her body had been found lying among the tombstones in the graveyard of the local church. She had been beaten about the head and strangled. Her clothing was disarranged and her breasts exposed. The right breast bore an unmistakeable bite mark.

William Muncie, who would later become Assistant Chief Constable of Strathclyde Police, led the murder investigation. Extensive house-to-house enquiries were made and a band of travelling showmen and a party of weekend caravanners were questioned. Filtering through a mass of statements, police began to focus their attention on a local boys' approved school where some thirty youths were boarders. Fifty officers were assigned to the case.

The bite mark on the murder victim was seen as a crucial piece of evidence. Muncie arranged for a photograph to be taken and sent to John Furness, Lecturer in Forensic Dentistry at the Police Training School in Liverpool. His opinion was that the mark could be used not only to identify the attacker but also to eliminate suspects from further enquiries. This view was corroborated by Dr. Warren Harvey, Consultant at the Glasgow Dental Hospital, who was currently on holiday. He offered to return at once to take dental impressions of any suspect the police referred to him.

By this time, the result of police enquiries led officers to question seventeen-year-old Gordon Hay, a boarder at the boys' school. A fellow pupil had admitted that he had lied to cover up his friend's absence from school late on the evening of 6 August. When Hay returned to his dormitory around 10.30, in a dishevelled and agitated state, he persuaded his room mates to say that they all had been in bed by lights out at 10.00 p.m.

The strategy adopted by William Muncie was to ask Dr. Harvey to take dental impressions of all the boys at the school, being careful not to tell him who his suspect was. Each impression taken was identified by a number. The photograph of the bite showed five marks with distinctive oval shapes which Harvey thought were too large to have been caused by a single tooth and had been made either by a sharp or jagged tooth or by two adjacent teeth. Using these criteria, and comparing the impressions with photographs of the bite, he was able to eliminate all but five of the impressions. He thought the most likely match was Number 14.

It was at this stage that Dr. Harvey thought it prudent to seek advice from a forensic pathologist and so he enlisted the help of Keith Simpson. He travelled to London with the five dental impressions and met Simpson at Guy's Hospital. After scrutinising the impressions, the pathologist opted for Number 14 as the most likely match. While they were in agreement, the two men had lingering doubts that the identification was strong enough to warrant an arrest.

For the moment, it was back to the drawing board. Then, Keith Simpson had a brainwave. Why not, he suggested, take further dental impressions of the five suspects and make new models in acrylic resin of both upper and lower sections which could be hinged and used to simulate a bite. As Simpson put it, rather prosaically, they could then make trial bites on the breast of a "suitable female body in the mortuary".

This they did but with disappointing results because the trial conclusively eliminated impression Number 14. Once again, it was back to the drawing board. Dr. Harvey doggedly set to work re-examining all the impressions and photographs, directing his attention in particular to two small dark spots which formed part of the bite left on the victim. He scoured the literature on bite marks but could find no guidance as to the kind of teeth that might leave such marks.

Minutely examining all the impressions, he finally found what he was looking for – marks left by upper and lower canine teeth, each of which contained minute hollow blemishes on the tip. These were evident only on impression Number 11. Harvey and Simpson now took a fresh look at the position of the attacker relative to his victim and determined that he had been positioned behind and leaned over her shoulder to bite her right breast. Drawing this new orientation into their thinking enabled them to see that impression

Number 11 was a perfect match to the bite on the body.

The scientific evidence backed up the circumstantial evidence against Gordon Hay which Muncie and his team had been accumulating. But still there were doubts because a minimum of four or five adjacent teeth corresponding with a bite mark were the benchmark established by the Swedish expert Dr. Gösta **Gustafson** whose textbook, *Forensic Odontology*, was the only published authority available at that time. So, Warren Harvey set about an exhaustive study of a thousand canine teeth in sample groups of boys aged between sixteen and seventeen.

He found only two with pits and none with two pits in the same mouth. He concluded that the pits in question were not due to dental caries or wear but to hypocalcination. Using state-of-the-art photography, he prepared transparencies of Gordon Hay's teeth and superimposed them on photographs of the bite marks on the victim's body. Keith Simpson said, "It is akin to tool-marking evidence or fingerprints". The evidence against Hay was now strong enough to warrant an arrest and he was duly charged with murder.

The testimony given by Dr. Harvey at the trial was a model of clarity and thoroughness. He modestly told the court, "I am not an expert". Keith Simpson testified that "In more than thirty years' practice, I have not seen a bite mark with better defined detail than this". The judge referred to forensic odontology as "a relatively new science" but acknowledged "there must, of course, always be a first time for everything". Indeed, it was the first time in Scotland that an individual had been charged with murder on the basis of bite mark evidence.

The jury found the result convincing and delivered a majority verdict of guilty. Thus was concluded a remarkable collaboration between pathologist and dentist which broke new ground in the evolving science of forensic dentistry. Not the least of their achievements was a demonstration of the significant role that dental evidence can play in eliminating innocent suspects from a criminal investigation.

A measure of how quickly things had moved on in this field was provided during the time of the troubles in Ireland in the 1970s. An incident occurred when a group of men were gunned down by an IRA hitman who threw away a partially-eaten apple as he made good his escape from the crime scene. When this was given to a forensic odontologist, he recognised a peculiarity in the bite mark which he believed had been made by an individual with a deformed jaw. He advised the police that this man had a lantern jaw and facial features which probably included a large nose, high forehead and thin, narrow face.

During a round-up of possible suspects, investigators found such an individual who agreed to have impressions taken of his teeth. A perfect match was found with the bite mark left on the apple. The man was sent for trial and convicted of murder. This incident showed what an experienced dentist could offer in terms of relating dental impressions to other individual identifying features such as face shape.

An apple featured as a prime exhibit in an arson case which made the headlines in 1976. John Furness, who had played a part in solving the Biggar murder, had by this time established himself as an authority on bite marks and, in addition to lecturing on forensic odontology at Liverpool University, had also been appointed a Home Office consultant. It was in this capacity that he answered a ring on his doorbell one day to be presented with a partially eaten apple by two police officers.

In the small hours of 3 April, a fire in Southport destroyed a large part of a building housing the offices of North West Water Board. After the blaze had been brought under control, investigators combed the burned out offices and, in one of them, found an apple with a single bite taken out of it. This was retrieved as a possible piece of evidence relating to the arson attack.

While John Furness was examining the Golden Delicious apple, police investigators were focussing on likely suspects which led them to the home of Karl Johnson. He was a Southport dustman with a criminal record but, when questioned, denied any involvement with the recent blaze. He did, though, agree to have impressions taken of his teeth.

Hot on the trail, John Furness found forty-six points of similarity between Johnson's dental impressions and the bite marks on the apple. This high degree of matching characteristics was judged to be as good as a fingerprint and Johnson was charged with arson. He was subsequently convicted and sentenced to three years' imprisonment in the first criminal case in Britain in which the sole evidence of identification was provided by a bite mark.

When the case came up for appeal in 1977, the validity of the dental evidence was severely tested. Johnson's legal representative sought to discredit forensic odontology as new, unreliable and little more than an interesting sideline. But he had reckoned without John Furness who was about to have his day in court. He demonstrated that the individual characteristics of Johnson's teeth had been perfectly replicated in the bite mark left on the apple found at the crime scene. He argued that in a case involving a full set of teeth, the odds against two people having identical impressions were on a par with fingerprints.

The odontologist explained that each individual has a singular pattern of wear to their teeth relating to chewing and mouth movements which form part of a unique dental history. Mr. Justice Mars-Jones, in dismissing the appeal remarked that forensic odontology was now an established science comparable with fingerprints and trace evidence.

An important development on the British scene was the publication in 1973 of *Forensic Dentistry* by Professor James **Cameron** and Bernard Sims. The aim of this work, as Keith Simpson noted in his foreword, was to advance the practice of forensic odontology for medico-legists, the police and the judiciary. Comparisons were inevitably made with Gustafson's book which had for several years been the only available work on the subject. But, as Cameron emphasised, his book was not in competition with what had gone before but was intended to be complementary.

As the world became more accustomed to dealing with death on a massive scale, caused by natural disasters, major transportation accidents and the atrocities of genocide, so the need to identify ravaged human remains grew in importance. Forensic odontology had developed into a highly specialised science and, allied to forensic anthropology, became the means by which the unnamed dead could be identified.

The reality of this specialised field of study has been told by Dr. William **Maples** in his book *Dead Men Do Tell Tales*, published in 1994. Maples headed the Human Identification Laboratory at the University of Florida. Among his graphic accounts is the story of three murders and a suicide which, though linked, were committed hundreds of miles apart and posed a conundrum that took eighteen months to unravel. But, two teeth found in different places provided the solution.

In January 1985, the bodies of a married couple were found dead in their home in New Hampshire, USA. Both in their forties, they had been stabbed to death and the house set on fire. Twelve days later, and many miles away in Gainseville, Florida, two bodies destroyed beyond immediate recognition, were found in a burnt out cabin. Near by was a car, traced to Glyde Meek and Paige Jennings. There was a suicide note which referred to the deaths of Paige's parents in New Hampshire.

Both incidents involved Meek, a man with a criminal record and, as it transpired, an instigator of family feuds. The question investigators asked concerned his whereabouts and was he one of the victims of the fire at Gainseville? Dr. Maples described the results of the fire which had reduced the two bodies to a crumbling mass of ash. Initial examination of these remains produced no evidence of identity. As enquiries progressed, Maples discovered that Meek had consulted a chiropractor for treatment of a back problem. As part of the examination, X-ray photographs had been taken of the patient's upper back, showing the rib cage. One of the X-rays was sufficiently extended into the lower neck and jaw to reveal that Meek had a gold tooth filling. Knowing that such a metal filling would be extremely resistant to high temperatures, prompted Maples to look again at the remains taken from the scene of the fire.

Everything was put through a fine sieve and a tooth with a gold filling came to light. Meek's dentist confirmed from his records that he had made a prominent gold filling in one of his teeth. While this was significant, it meant little on its own but, during a search of Meek's car, detectives had found a match box containing a normal, healthy tooth which contained a filling. Again, the dentist confirmed from his records that this was indeed a tooth from Meek's mouth.

By means of the two teeth, it was possible to confirm that Glyde Meek had died in the fire. Piecing all the crime scene evidence together, it seemed that Meek murdered his girlfriend's parents and torched their home in an effort to destroy evidence and then drove to Florida where he killed his girlfriend, set their cabin on fire and shot himself dead. So, the riddle of three murders and a suicide were solved by two teeth and some persistent dental detective work.

John Furness, a distinguished forensic odontologist, summed up rather neatly when he said "You can lie through your teeth, but your teeth cannot lie".

HATCHED AND MATCHED

Forensic Entomology

The late comedian Frankie Howerd famously remarked about a joke made at a legal hearing that "a titter ran round the court". Such was the case at Gloucester Assizes in 1965 when Quintin Hogg QC put a question to an expert witness during a murder trial.

In the course of a somewhat eccentric bout of cross-examination regarding evidence of insect activity on the victim's corpse, he put a proposition to Professor Alfred McKenny-Hughes, a distinguished entomologist, "let us suppose," he said, "that the bluebottle lays its eggs on the dead body at midnight on the….". "Oh, dear me, no!", interjected the professor, "no self-respecting bluebottle lays eggs at midnight". This response produced stifled laughter and a subsequent talking point about the egg-laying activities of *Calliphora erythrocephalus*.

Until the late 1600s, it was commonly believed that maggots which appeared on rotting meat were spontaneously generated. It was not until 1668 that Francesco Redi, an Italian physician, confirmed the connection between flies, the eggs they laid and the maggots, or larvae, which resulted.

In the following century, attempts were made to identify the insects which infested decomposing human remains. And there were glimmerings of a new science on the horizon – forensic entomology. An important advance in these studies was made in 1855 by Louis François Étienne **Bergeret**, a French doctor working in the mountain town of d'Arbois.

In the course of his duties, Dr. Bergeret was called on to carry out a post mortem on the mummified body of a child which had been discovered walled up behind a mantelpiece in the room of a house in Paris.

He noted evidence of insect activity on the corpse and made special note of the pattern of succession related to the duration of life cycles of the different species which infested the body. By analysing this evidence, he was able to work out that the child had died seven years before its body was discovered. In consequence, the police were prompted to investigate the tenants of the house in 1848, and in due course, arrested two people who were later convicted of murdering the child.

Bergeret's achievement was to show that it was possible to calculate the post mortem interval from the succession pattern of insects on a corpse. These were the beginnings of what would become forensic entomology. The next step was made by another French scientist and, by coincidence, involved the semi-mummified body of a child.

Jean Pierre **Mégnin** was a military veterinarian who had made a particular study of insect life on animal corpses. His speciality was skin diseases and the treatment of dogs for parasitic mites. It was in this capacity that he was invited in 1878 to give an opinion regarding the death of an infant whose abandoned body was found by the roadside in Paris. A feature noted by Dr. Mégnin when he carried out a post mortem was that the corpse was covered with mites. By analysing the type and scale of insect activity, he was able to advise the pathologist that death had probably occurred at least six months before the body was discovered.

Having established his special credentials, Mégnin was called on to assist the police in other investigations and his reputation continued to grow. As he extended his knowledge and experience, he saw a new science emerging and turned his attention to the life cycle of blowflies and the possibilities that insect activity could provide accurate indications of the post mortem interval. In 1894, he published a seminal study entitled, *La Faune des Cadavres*, and forensic entomology was given a sound scientific basis.

There were, though, some contemporary scientists who did not believe Mégnin's work should be taken too seriously. This scepticism was not shared by medico-legal practitioners who saw immense possibilities in this new method of calculating time of death. Mégnin extended the scope of his studies to include all the variables that affected insect populations on a decaying corpse, such as temperature, climate, time of year, ground conditions and other factors. By the time of his death in 1905, the principle that post mortem interval could be determined by analysing insect activity, and especially faunal succession, had become established practice.

As bodies left in the open start to decompose, they attract flies, commonly of the bluebottle family, which lay eggs in the natural openings of the body, chiefly the mouth and nose. If the corpse is unclothed, the anus and genitals may also be targeted, as they offer moist conditions favoured by flies. Any areas of broken skin caused, for example, by knife or gunshot wounds also attract insects.

As the eggs hatch out to maggots in three stages, a process which may taken ten to twelve days, the decomposing corpse becomes a feeding ground for a seething mass of larvae. It is the chronicling of these life cycles which provides entomologists with the information by which they can determine the time that has elapsed since the victim died – the post mortem interval. Maggots feed off soft tissues at an alarming rate and can destroy a corpse within days, especially in warm weather conditions.

Forensic entomology played an important part in the investigation of a double murder in Britain in 1935. In September of that year, a woman out walking, crossed a bridge at the Edinburgh-Carlisle road near Moffat. As she did so, she glanced down into the stream below and noticed something strange by the water's edge. She saw what she believed to be a human arm wrapped around with newspaper.

Police were called to the scene and extensive searches turned up a gruesome collection of body parts. Aside from identifying the remains, an important question was to establish how long they had been lying where they were found. Professor John **Glaister**, the Glasgow forensic pathologist, had the grisly task of examining the remains and trying to piece them together.

He found maggots feeding on the rotting flesh and collected a few specimens which he referred to his Glasgow colleague, Professor Alexander Mearns, who was an entomologist. The maggots were identified as blowfly larvae and, from the stage of development they had reached, and allowing up to two days for the insects to find the remains, he judged they were between twelve and fourteen days old. This estimate exactly corresponded with another discovery. A newspaper used to wrap some of the body parts had been retrieved and seen to bear the date, 15 September. It had been published in Lancaster. From this information, investigators were able to establish the date and place of the murders.

While the pathologists were reassembling more than seventy body parts into two distinct individuals, police were questioning Dr. Buck Ruxton, a local medical practitioner. He had the anatomical skills necessary to have disarticulated the bodies and forensic searches discovered ample evidence of blood-letting in his house. Significantly, the doctor had reported cutting his hand on 15 September and getting blood on his clothes. This was the day on which he wielded a knife in the process of dismembering his victims, one of whom was his wife, and cutting his hand.

The evidence provided by the blowfly maggots suggested 15 September was the day that murder visited Dr. Ruxton's house. In a subsequent written confession he acknowledged that he had killed his wife "in a fit of temper" and also her friend, Mary Rogerson.

Buoyed-up by what he regarded as unchallengeable evidence, Professor Glaister discussed with lawyers the significance of the blowfly larvae and spoke of his intention to use it in his trial testimony. This idea was rejected, though, because the prosecution lawyers did not think the jury would stomach talk about maggots and certainly not the sight of pickled larvae in a glass bottle.

In the event, Buck Ruxton was convicted on a wealth of groundbreaking scientific evidence. The maggots which had helped to confirm the date on which he committed the murders were consigned to history and hidden from a squeamish jury. Consequently, the otherwise authoritative account of the trial, in *The Notable British Trials* series, carries no reference to Professor Mearns and his work on the maggots. This was perhaps an indication that entomology would be regarded as something of a poor relation in the spectrum of forensic sciences. Indeed, the "bug doctors" of later years became used to dealing with corpses that were so grossly decomposed that pathologists could achieve little by examining the remains and were keen to pass them on.

Not many people go out searching for maggots but this was the mission two boys set themselves on 28 June 1964. Their aim was to patrol the woods near their home in Bracknell, Berkshire, in the hope of finding a recently dead animal that harboured some maggots. The intention was to gather a few larvae to use as fishing bait, something which they had done several time previously.

The boys' search was rewarded when they spotted a mass of bloated white maggots on a grassy mound. They pulled at the grass to free up their catch and, in doing so, exposed a rotting piece of flesh which they recognised as a human forearm.

Police were called to the scene and it quickly became apparent that a shallow grave containing a human body had been found in Bracknell Woods. Pathologist, Professor Keith **Simpson**, was called out and took samples of the maggots which he assumed to be bluebottles, or *Calliphora erythrocephalus*. He knew that in warm, summer weather, the fly eggs hatched very quickly and judged that the maggots had probably hatched nine to ten days previously. Allowing time for the bluebottles to seek out the dead body, meant that the individual, whose remains lay before him, had died on 16 or 17 June. Being an astute observer of a potential crime scene, Simpson noticed that beech cuttings had been used to cover the shallow burial site. He thought this was odd as there were no beech trees in the woods.

At post mortem, it was clear from the broken bones in the larynx that the man had been killed by a blow to the throat. He was aged between forty and fifty years and was of small stature standing at around five feet three or four inches. But who was he? Detectives had been scouring missing persons files from which they ascertained that Peter Thomas had disappeared from his home in Gloucestershire on 16 June. He was a man with a police record and his fingerprints were on file. These matched the prints of the dead man found in the woods.

It was discovered that, despite living in poor circumstances, Thomas had made a loan of £2,000 to a man named William Brittle who lived in Hampshire. Significantly, the loan was due to be repaid in June 1964. When questioned by detectives, Brittle said he had driven the hundred and forty miles to Thomas's home on 16 June to settle the debt. On his return journey, he claimed to have picked up a hitchhiker who would be able to confirm the date and route.

At this point, the investigation into Thomas's death began to founder. Firstly, the hitchhiker confirmed that Brittle had given him a lift and, secondly, a man came forward to report that he had seen Peter Thomas in Gloucester on 20 June. If this was so, suspicion against Brittle began to evaporate because the sighting ran counter to the timing provided by the maggots on the corpse. Adding to the doubts were two further claims by witnesses who said they had seen Thomas on 21 June.

Professor Simpson who had made a special study of time of death evidence was prepared to stake his reputation on his calculations that Thomas had died on 16 or 17 June. After the Director of Public Prosecutions declined to pursue the case against Brittle, a Coroner's inquest held at Bracknell came to a different conclusion and decided he should be tried for murder.

A forensic examination of Brittle's car had turned up little that was incriminating beyond a solitary beech leaf which at least gave a circumstantial connection with the grave site. It was also discovered that Brittle had taken an unarmed combat course while in the army which would have given him the expertise to deliver a karate chop to the victim's throat likely to break the bones in his larynx.

William Brittle was tried for murder at Gloucester in 1965. His defence team had secured the services of a distinguished entomologist, Professor McKenny-Hughes, whom Simpson thought might contest his evidence. In an eccentric performance, the entomologist entertained the court with some maggoty tales. They are "curious little devils", he said, and producing a matchbox, from his pocket, he continued, "… suppose you have a hundred maggots here, ninety-nine will make their way to the body, but the hundredth little devil, he'll turn the other way".

Possibly to Keith Simpson's relief, the professor did not challenge his interpretation of the entomological evidence. The outcome was that Brittle was convicted of murder and given a life sentence. Simpson's reputation remained intact and he had emphatically endorsed the credibility of gauging time of death from insect activity on the corpse.

The attractions of forensic entomology were slow to take root in America after the advances made in Europe. This was, perhaps, unsurprising, as the insect population in the New World with its proliferation of indigenous species, was a world away from that across the Atlantic.

That is not to say that entomology was a lost cause, just that there were different priorities. First and foremost was the need to develop scientific means of protecting America's agriculture industry from insect-born pestilence. To this end, pockets of expertise were established, usually by individual enthusiasts, identifying species and working out taxonomic strategies. The entomologists did not always command the respect they deserved but their persistence was rewarded in 1881 when the government set up an entomology laboratory in Washington DC.

It would be another fifty years before the scientific investigation of crime in the USA was put on a firm foundation. The FBI opened its crime laboratory in 1932 when J. Edgar Hoover, the Bureau's director, enthusiastically embraced scientific methods in the pursuit of criminals. Yet, forensic entomology, with all its potential for measuring the important parameters of time of death, remained an outsider. A further three decades passed before a US entomologist would be called on to give scientific evidence in a murder trial.

Despite some notable successes using the new methods of determining post mortem interval, recognition of the potential was slow to materialise. In 1965, Jerry Payne in South Carolina published the results of his pioneering work on decomposition. Using pig carcasses as his research medium, he compared the results obtained from studies of two groups – carcasses that were exposed to insect activity and those that were not.

Payne's landmark research, while applauded by his contemporaries, passed largely unnoticed by the wider scientific community. He had, though, put down a marker which would lead to the USA taking a pre-eminent position in the use of forensic entomology as a means of establishing time of death with hitherto unheard of accuracy.

The next logical step was to graduate from animals to humans to carry this research forward. This occurred in 1981 under the direction of William **Bass**, Professor of Anthropology at the University of Tennessee at Knoxville. A seasoned practitioner,

Bill Bass, set up the Anthropological Research Facility (ARF), more popularly referred to as "The Body Farm". Unidentified and unclaimed bodies were donated for this unique research programme which aimed to monitor the process of natural decomposition. Some bodies were left exposed to the elements, while others were put in shallow graves. "The Body Farm" was described as the only place in the world where the symbiosis between corpses and insect activity could be observed through every cycle.

Bass's initiative also showed the benefits to be achieved with various branches of forensic science working together; anthropology, botany and entomology. An example of what could be achieved was demonstrated by a missing person enquiry in August 1984.

A young woman was reported absent from her home in Falls Church, Virginia, following a disagreement with her boyfriend. When her sandals were found in a wooded area outside the town, her family organised an extensive search of the area which resulted in the discovery of her body. Although only a week had elapsed since her disappearance, the body was in an advanced state of decomposition and infested with maggots to the extent that the medical examiner was unable to ascertain cause of death. The body was released for burial.

Having viewed the state of the corpse, one of the investigators decided to send photographs, together with some preserved maggots, to a forensic entomologist for an opinion. The entomologist, one of Bill Bass's team, was struck by the advanced state of decomposition and the fact that the chest and hands seemed to have been targeted. His experience told him that this looked like differential decomposition, when maggots feed on parts of the body other than the natural moist openings. His assessment was that this intense maggot infestation indicated the presence of bleeding due to injury. The train of thought was that the girl had probably been stabbed and suffered defensive wounds on her hands in the process.

An exhumation followed, when pathologists found knife cuts on the sternum and ribs, indicative of stabbing with a thin-bladed knife, and also nicks on the bones of her hands strongly suggesting defensive wounds. Clearly, a murder had been committed and death resulted from stab wounds. No firm case could be brought against any of the suspects, so the young woman's murder remained unsolved.

What the episode had demonstrated was that using the new research, scientists were able to probe the secrets of death and reconstruct a corpse's history. Bill Bass, widely regarded as the founding father of forensic anthropology, was still working in his seventies and, in 2003, published a memoir appropriately entitled, *Death's Acre*.

He had been instrumental in bringing the new forensic sciences in from the periphery and entomology was one of these. He inspired others through his teaching and led the USA into new realms of thinking about time of death which, together with cause of death, were two of the most frequently asked questions in a murder enquiry.

Another innovator about to make his mark in this arcane field of science was M. Lee **Goff**, a zoology graduate who took up entomology at the University of Hawaii. He soon found himself called on by law enforcement agencies to assist with their investigations and, in due course, became Professor of Forensic Entomology.

In 2000, Professor Goff published a comprehensive account of his subject which he called *A Fly For The Prosecution*. This book opened up the subject to a wide readership. He capitalised on the work of generations of taxonomists, identifying and classifying a myriad of insect forms. His gift was to realise that some of nature's humblest life forms had the capacity to teach us a great deal. Goff introduced his readers to a wonderful galaxy of insect forms including the red-legged ham beetle, the black soldier fly and the cheese skipper. Here was a world apart from the dry Latin names which were the stock-in-trade of bug hunters.

Across a range of crime cases offering different challenges, he consistently showed the value of forensic entomology in determining the all important post mortem interval. In June 1996, the clothed body of a US marine was found by the roadside in Honolulu. The man had been shot and his body rolled down a grassy slope. Fellow marines were suspected of the killing which followed a disagreement over a debt.

Professor Goff took soil and vegetation samples from the crime scene and collected specimens of many species of fly larvae and also adult beetles active on the corpse. He made calculations from this evidence and also from the ground conditions. Recent rainfall combined with a cocoon of canvas wrapping that had been put round the body kept the corpse moist and allowed more than one generation of maggots to develop.

Taking everything into consideration, the entomologist put the post mortem interval at 29 to 31 days. This proved to be a remarkably reliable estimate when the perpetrators of the assault on the marine confessed to their crime which had occurred 30 days before the body was discovered.

A new dimension pioneered by US entomologists was the discovery that maggots absorb drugs from the body tissues they feed on. Hence, when a body is found in an advanced state of decomposition and practically reduced to a skeleton, maggots feeding on it can be analysed for drugs as if they were part of the soft tissues. In these circumstances the maggots can be tested as if they were extensions of the body. This was a development that can have a bearing on determining cause of death when reasons may otherwise be obscure.

Professor Goff led from the front in establishing forensic entomology as more than a fringe activity. Indeed his efforts were instrumental in persuading the FBI to include it in its training courses. Agents now routinely look for and record insect activity at crime scenes and secure maggots as part of their evidence collection.

The leading British forensic entomologist in the late 1980s was Dr. Zakaria **Erzinclioglu**, popularly known as 'Zak', who trained as a zoologist. His speciality was blowflies.

'Zak's' expertise was valued by the police, particularly after his findings when an unidentified body was found in Cardiff in 1989. By identifying the insect evidence on the body and the surroundings in which it was discovered, he calculated that the person had been dead for five years. This put the year of death at 1984 and enabled the police to narrow the search through missing person's files. The body was identified as that of a girl who had gone missing in 1981.

'Maggot' is one of those words not frequently used in polite society because of the images it invokes. 'Zak' demythologised the subject with his matter-of-fact approach which earned him the title, 'maggotologist', from the investigators with whom he worked.

READING THE BONES

Forensic Anthropology

"In memory of an unknown man". This was the epitaph of an unidentified murder victim whose remains were buried in an English churchyard in 1930. Late on Bonfire Night in that year, the life of an unnamed man was consumed by a car fire in what became known as "The Blazing Car Mystery". While the victim remained unknown, the perpetrator, Alfred Arthur Rouse, became infamous.

While driving to Leicester, Rouse stopped to pick up a hitchhiker. During the journey, he stopped the car in order to answer a call of nature. He asked his passenger to refill the fuel tank using a spare can of petrol. Minutes later, the car was engulfed in a sea of flames with the passenger trapped inside.

Two men passing by attempted a rescue but were defeated by the intensity of the fire. Rouse, meanwhile, had abandoned the scene and was later traced by the police. Once the fire was extinguished, the charred remains of the car occupant were taken away for examination by Dr. Eric Shaw, a local GP and pathologist. The body had been reduced to part of the head, some of the trunk and portions of limbs.

A post mortem was carried out at Northampton General Hospital by renowned pathologist, Sir Bernard **Spilsbury**. He and Dr. Shaw attempted to establish some identifying features of the fire victim. The remains of a prostate gland determined the gender as male, while the appearance of the bones suggested an adult person around 5ft 8 inches in height. The state of the teeth indicated an age of around thirty years.

Charged with murder, Rouse was put on trial and a jury convicted him. He was executed in March 1931 and his confession appeared in a newspaper the following day. He explained that he had strangled the hitchhiker and set fire to the car to feign his own death. The identity of his victim was never established, despite the best efforts of the pathologists of the day.

"The Blazing Car Mystery" highlighted the difficulties faced in identifying individuals consumed by fire and posed challenges for the newly developing science of forensic anthropology. This involves the study of variations in anatomy of the human body, especially the skeletal structure. It is a discipline that has become increasingly important in the modern world faced with both natural and man-made disasters. Earthquakes, wars, genocide, air crashes, fires and explosions leave a trail of death and destruction with a toll of victims to be identified.

Forensic anthropology has its origins in the USA and the insight of Professor Thomas **Dwight**, who, in 1878, highlighted the possibility of identifying the remains of long dead individuals by examining the bones of their skeletons.

One of the pioneers of this developing science in Europe was Professor Karl **Pearson** who devised a formula for calculating the height of an individual by measuring the long bones. This was an important development in the quest to establish human identity from skeletal remains.

When human relics are discovered, frequently unearthed from unmarked graves, the first priority is identification. Crucial elements of this process are to determine the gender, age and height of the individual. Gender may be ascertained by examining the pelvic bones on the basis that the child-bearing capacity of a woman requires a broader pelvis. This means that the female pelvis has a wider angle between the pubic symphyses. The skull and long bones may also be used to determine gender.

Age may be judged from the morphological changes in young individuals such as bone fusion and developments in dentition. In older people, the state of the teeth, particularly patterns of wear, are significant. Height of the individual can be assessed by measuring the long bones of the skeleton.

Racial origin is the most difficult to establish, although there are differences in morphology of the skull between individuals of European origin and those of African descent which may help. There is a tendency towards prognathism in the latter and flat features may indicate an individual of Mongoloid origin. Disease and occupational wear and tear often leave traces on the bones and healed bone fractures can provide important indicators of identity.

When only partial remains are discovered, the first task of the anthropologist is to determine whether they are human or animal. This depends on the shape and character of individual bones which enable an experienced examiner to tell the difference. Where practicable, re-assembly of scattered bones into a skeletal form is a key factor.

Human relics are sometimes found where the head has been obliterated, either by disaster or criminal activity, with the result that identification is not possible. Thanks to forensic modelling techniques pioneered in the 1900s by Ales **Hrdlicka**, this problem can be overcome.

In 1993, the headless body of an unidentified man was found in a Manchester street. He remained anonymous until a severed head was discovered at a different location and matched to the body. Identification was still not possible because the head and facial features had been deliberately smashed beyond recognition.

A specialist in facial modelling and reconstruction was consulted and the head was remodelled to show how it would have looked in life. Photographs were published in the media with the result that the murdered man was identified by someone who had known him as a professional colleague.

An important aspect of forensic anthropology is dentistry which brings its own speciality to the task of identification. The state of dental wear and upkeep are unique to every individual and when compared with records of dental treatment can provide clinching evidence of identity. Forensic anthropology allied to odontology has been used extensively to identify victims of wars, genocide and disasters of many kinds.

A FORENSIC FORUM

In 1993, in Waco, Texas, a ranch owned by the Branch Davidians, a religious sect which followed the teachings of David Koresh, was consumed by an intense fire. Following a shoot-out with FBI agents, survivors of the fire called off their resistance, allowing the consequences of the catastrophe to be investigated. The authorities were faced with the task of recovering and identifying the remains of those who had perished. A wide range of forensic disciplines was called upon.

Using basic biological profiling techniques, including fingerprinting, DNA and dental records, body parts were re-assembled to determine the number of deaths which had occurred. Eighty-six bodies were identified, including that of David Koresh who had been shot in the head before being consumed in the fire.

A leading anthropologist in the 1970s was Dr. William **Bass** who pioneered research on the subject by setting up facilities known as "body farms". These were designed to further scientific understanding of the processes which govern the destruction of buried bodies. The protocols established proved to be of immense value in resolving historical deaths where doubts had surfaced about the circumstances.

One such case was the death of US President Zachary Taylor in 1850. He had been in office for just over a year when he died, aged sixty-six, supposedly of food poisoning. Doubts about the true cause of death surfaced periodically and there were suspicions that Taylor had been killed with poison on account of the position he had taken on slavery.

When doubts re-emerged in the 1990s, permission was given to exhume President Taylor's body and use modern methods to determine the true cause of death. This task fell to Dr. William Maples, Head of the Human Identification Laboratory at the University of Florida. He confronted the remains of the former President when they were retrieved from the vault in the National Cemetery in Louisville, Kentucky, where they had lain undisturbed for a hundred and forty years.

The body had been reduced to a skeleton with hair still attached to the scalp. With its retentive power to store traces of poison, the hair was particularly significant. A detailed anthropological examination was made of the remains and Dr. Maples analysed samples of hair and fingernails for poison. His tests indicated the presence of small amounts of arsenic which toxicologists confirmed were entirely consistent with normal body levels. As such, they could not have caused illness or death by poisoning. Hence, Zachary Taylor had not been a victim of assassination, but, in all probability, had succumbed to a bout of food poisoning.

Describing his work, Dr. Maples, who had acquired the accolade of being a "bone detective", expressed the wish that the work he carried out as a forensic anthropologist would be "a discipline useful to society". He proved the point when he began working to help identify unaccounted for military personnel lost in the Vietnam War and other fields of conflict.

Human remains repatriated to the USA often amounted to just a handful of bones, frequently mixed with those of animal origin. A preliminary task was to put aside any non-human bones and focus on the remainder in an endeavour to determine the basics of identification – age, sex, height and race. A great deal of cross-checking was needed before an identity could be verified enabling a grieving family to be notified. The presence of teeth among remains assisted the process and forensic odontologists were essential members of the investigating teams.

In 2015, the remains of a US serviceman lost for over half a century, were identified by means of dental records. The skeleton of a marine was found on a Pacific island where he had been killed fighting the Japanese in 1943. Identification was made by comparing the dentition of the remains with a data bank of dental records. This was a prime example of the principle that time is no barrier to the work of the forensic anthropologist.

In another domain, that of identifying victims of murderous activity, the Jeffrey Dahmer case is instructive. When Dahmer, the cannibal serial killer, known as "Chop Chop Man", admitted killing and dismembering seventeen people, the first task of investigators was to identify the victims. A search of his apartment in Milwaukee resulted in the discovery of numerous body parts. There, investigators found seven skulls, four severed heads and assorted human remains in the refrigerator and freezer. A collection of assorted body parts, including a number of hacked off limbs, was found in a large barrel.

Attention next focussed on the land adjoining the Milwaukee property. Five complete skeletons were unearthed, together with assorted bone fragments and teeth, amounting to over two hundred separate items. Animal bones were separated from those of human origin which were sent to the Smithsonian Institution in Washington for detailed analysis.

One group of bones was confirmed as originating from a single individual. Scientists were able to determine the age, height and gender of a young adult whom Dahmer had claimed as his first victim in 1978. Dahmer explained that he had killed the man in his flat and dismembered the body. He put the remains in plastic bags which he then buried. Later, he disinterred the parts and smashed them to pieces with a sledgehammer. Even this act of destruction did not defeat the work of the anthropologists. In due course, Dahmer was judged guilty of murder and given fifteen life sentences. In 1994, he was attacked and killed by a fellow prison inmate.

Forensic anthropology has become an indispensable tool aiding the identification of victims subjected to every calamity ranging from murder to earthquakes. Dr. Cyril Wecht, a distinguished US pathologist, put it in a matter-of-fact way when he wrote, "Official, governmental medico-legal investigation of violent and suspicious deaths is an essential component of the criminal justice system".

The unique role of the anthropologist is to retrieve human identities even when bodies have been reduced to skeletal fragments. In a world prone to both natural and man-made disasters, often involving multiple deaths, the skills of the anthropologist help to dispel uncertainties and provide closure to previously unsolvable questions.

PUSHING UP THE DAISIES

Forensic Botany

Sir Arthur Conan **Doyle** is credited with many achievements, among them being hailed as the "Father of Forensic Science". Certainly, his great detective, Sherlock Holmes, had insights into many scientific disciplines and acknowledged their relevance to the arts of crime detection. Among them was a passing interest in botany, to the extent that, according to Dr. Watson, Holmes occasionally consulted a botanical reference book. One of the detective's special gifts was to ascertain an individual's movements by examining his boots and, most particularly, the soil and vegetation which clung to them.

With customary prescience, Holmes observed in *The Five Orange Pips* that, "it is not impossible… that a man should possess all knowledge which is likely to be useful to him in his work". This was a good operating principle for any professional and certainly for crime investigation. Although Watson noted that Holmes's proficiency in botany was "variable" and his chemistry was "eccentric".

Having sown the seed, it was only a matter of time before the real world caught up with Conan Doyle's fiction. A pioneer, in what would evolve as forensic botany, was an entrepreneurial German chemist. Dr. Georg **Popp** ran a business in Frankfurt which, among a range of commercial laboratory testing procedures, offered technical investigations into crime. He came onto the scene in the early 1900s at a time when science was beginning to make a significant impact on the development of fingerprint identification and analysis of trace evidence. Crucially, he foresaw the important part that microscopy would play in implementing the new advances.

In 1904, Dr. Popp was asked to assist the police in Freiburg who were investigating the murder of a woman who had been strangled and left in a field. Suspicion focussed on Karl Laubach, a Foreign Legionnaire, who, when questioned, strenuously denied any involvement in the woman's death. Scrapings taken from beneath his fingernails told another story. Fibres were found which matched microscopically the cloth of the scarf used to strangle the murder victim.

When Popp observed soil clinging to the bottom of Laubach's trousers, he again reached for his microscope. He found that the soil contamination came from the same source as the crime scene. Significantly, he also matched traces of vegetation from the murder scene which had transferred to the killer's clothing. Laubach eventually admitted his crime and was put on trial for murder.

Dr. Popp presented his forensic evidence to a Freiburg Court which found the man in the dock guilty as charged. The verdict was given wide coverage in the newspapers and Popp was treated as a celebrity. In a lecture to a learned society that year, he echoed Conan Doyle's earlier observations by emphasising the importance of allying scientific disciplines to the ends of justice. In this context, he specifically mentioned botany.

The forensic expert's fame reached new heights in 1921 when he solved the riddle of two town mayors who were murdered while out walking in the hills around Heidelberg. Concerns were raised when the two men failed to return to their homes. Suspicion fell on a man who had left a briefcase behind at his lodgings. This was searched when the discovery was reported to the police and correspondence addressed to one of the mayors was found in it. The man, identified as Leonard Siefert, was questioned and said that the letters must have been placed in his bag without his knowledge. A couple of weeks later, the bodies of the missing mayors were found in a wooded hillside. One had been shot and the other bludgeoned to death. Nearby, police investigators found what they believed to be a hideout used to stage an ambush.

At this point, Dr. Popp was called in to assist the police. He examined the hideout and assembled a collection of vegetation, including several varieties of moss and grass. While Siefert continued to deny any involvement, examination of his clothing told a different story. Traces of vegetation on his clothes matched that found in the hideout where Siefert had lain in wait to take his victims unaware.

Popp's evidence once again proved decisive. He had shown the range of possibilities which botanical evidence offered investigators in matching a suspect to a crime scene. Botanists were able to identify many different grass types down to specific varieties and minutiae such as leaf shape and even individual arrangement of plant cells. Allied to the powers of the microscope, botany was proving to be a potent addition to the range of forensic sciences available to the crime investigator.

Over the next twenty years Georg Popp's expertise was regularly sought when there was a prospect of trace evidence aiding a criminal investigation. He also became a mentor for aspiring forensic scientists as German influence in this field expanded. Centres of expertise had become established in several universities and researchers were inspired by Dr. Hans **Gross**, the Austrian criminologist, who published his authoritative work, *System Der Kriminalistik* in 1893.

The emphasis on scientific methods of investigating crime, pioneered in Europe, were quickly taken up in America. Joseph **Faurot**, a detective in the New York Police Department, urged his superiors to adopt fingerprinting after Scotland Yard had shown the way. And Dr. Edward **Heinrich**, like Popp, a criminological entrepreneur, embraced the potential offered by trace evidence. Heinrich became an advisor to police departments throughout the USA and achieved national recognition in 1923 when he solved a bungled train robbery in which three men had been shot dead.

A Southern Pacific express heading for San Francisco was held up by a group of armed men in the Siskiyou Mountains. The train was set on fire after the mail coach was blown apart with dynamite and three railway men were killed while the would be robbers escaped empty-handed.

A FORENSIC FORUM

Among the articles found at the crime scene was a pair of blue denim overalls which were given to Heinrich when he was called in to help the investigating officers. This discarded item of clothing provided a kaleidoscope of information and, after meticulous examination, and to the amazement of the investigators, he was able to provide a virtual description of the individual who had worn them.

The criminologist said they should be looking for a man aged around twenty, five feet ten inches tall, left-handed, with light brown hair who rolled his own cigarettes. All this, he divined by minutely examining the overalls. He analysed stains on the denim as pitch from fir trees and, in the pockets, found remnants of needles shed by Douglas fir trees. This enabled Heinrich to say that the owner of the overalls had worked as a lumberjack at one of the logging camps in the Pacific Northwest.

Putting together all the information gathered at the scene, crime investigators identified Roy d'Autrement as the man they were looking for. He was eventually brought to justice, following a nationwide manhunt, and was one of three brothers who had attacked the train. The outcome was a triumph for Edward Heinrich, and his methods earned him the title of, "The Edison of Crime Detection". He went on to become Professor of Criminology at Berkeley where he inspired a new generation of aspiring crime scientists. Like his European contemporaries, Heinrich emphasised that no criminal quits a crime scene without leaving traceable evidence behind. This would be the raison d'être for future crime scene investigation, or CSI, as it would become universally known.

One of America's most celebrated crime cases was the kidnapping in 1932 of the Lindbergh baby. The twenty-month-old boy whose father was Charles A. Lindbergh, the acclaimed aviator, was taken from his home in New Jersey and a ransom demanded for his release. Two months later, the boy's body was found in a shallow grave a few miles from the Lindbergh home.

While a nationwide hunt was mounted to find the kidnapper, scientists were examining the homemade ladder used to gain access to the upper floor of the house. Arthur **Koehler**, described as a "wood detective", or 'xylotomist', and a veteran of the US Forest Service, was asked to help detectives in this high profile case. He had made studies of cellular structure and growth rings in trees and had a reputation for identifying wood fragments and timber featuring in crime scene evidence.

Koehler set to work with the object of tracing the source of the wood used to construct the kidnap ladder. He identified the timber as run-of-the-mill pinewood and noted that the maker of the ladder had run out of material and finished his task by using a piece of floorboard. One of the "wood detective's" special talents was the interpretation of tool marks. He found that the timber of the ladder had been planed using a machine with a defect in one of its blades. This left characteristic marks on every piece of wood run through the machine. From his knowledge of the timber mills and the equipment they used, Koehler identified the yard in South Carolina which had machined the wood used to construct the ladder.

There was no record of the purchaser but, by then, police enquiries had led them to suspect Bruno Hauptmann, a German immigrant who had entered the USA illegally in 1923. Some of the ransom money was found in his possession. A visit to Hauptmann's home in the Bronx provided Koehler with a wealth of evidence. He found nail holes punched into the floor of the attic which exactly matched the nails in part of the ladder. He also discovered where a piece of the attic floor boarding had been taken up to provide the extra piece of timber needed in constructing the ladder.

In due course, Hauptmann was tried for the kidnap and murder of Charles Lindbergh Junior. His defence attorney mocked the idea of a "wood expert" testifying in court, declaring that is was not a science at all. The proceedings attracted great public attention and, having been judged guilty, Hauptmann went to the electric chair.

While the efforts of forensic botanists in the 1930s may, to some, have appeared amateurish, they were important stepping stones in the drive to extend the range of investigative skills available to police forces. In the ensuing decades, major advances would be made and some baffling criminal conundrums solved.

A man walking his dogs in New York's Central Park on a November day in 1942 allowed them off the leash to roam at will. The dogs made a beeline for an area that was being freshly landscaped and began sniffing and scuffing at the ground. When their owner caught up with them, he realised they had discovered the corpse of a young woman.

The body bore no identification and an autopsy confirmed that the woman, in her early twenties, had been strangled. The police searched Missing Persons files and came across a report of a twenty-three year old woman who had disappeared after going out on a weekend date. She was Louisa Almodovar who had been briefly married and then separated from her husband against a background of jealousy and alleged infidelity. Detectives learned that there had been friction between Terry Almodovar and his wife's parents. When questioned, he said that he had been out dancing on the night in question and that several of his dance partners could vouch for his alibi, which they did.

When Almodovar was searched, a pawn ticket was found in his pocket. He explained that this was for a green suit which he had recently worn. The suit was retrieved by detectives who tested it for bloodstains but with negative results. The garment was then passed on to Dr. Alexander O. **Gettler**, the toxicologist at the Medical Examiner's office. He noticed patches of soil clinging to the cloth and carried out spectrographic analysis on them. When these were compared with samples of soil taken from the crime scene, he found that they matched. Almodovar continued to protest his innocence but the police believed they had sufficient evidence to charge him with murder.

Grass seeds had been found in the suspect's trouser turn-ups and Dr. Gettler thought these merited detailed scrutiny. To assist him, he called on the services of Professor Joseph J. Copeland, a botanist at City College. Putting the seeds under his microscope, he made a significant discovery. Firstly, he identified them as a species with a compelling name, *Panicum dichoth milleflorium*, and, secondly, he reported that this was a very rare type of grass. So rare, in fact, that it grew in only three places within a ten-mile radius of Central Park. One of these places was the small hillock in the Park where Louisa Almodovar's body was found.

Confronted with this damning evidence which, contrary to his denial, placed Terry Almodovar in Central Park, he suddenly remembered that he had made a visit there in September. This might have worked, but for the additional insight provided by Professor Copeland. He told investigators that one of the features of

Panicum dichoth milleflorium was that if flowered late and did not produce seeds before mid-October.

Almodovar had done his best to outwit the police which included withdrawing an earlier confession when he admitted killing his wife in a fit of rage. He was found guilty of murder on the basis of the incontrovertible botanical evidence which had placed him at the crime scene.

A tragic incident that gave forensic botany international prominence was the kidnapping and murder of an eight-year-old boy in Australia in 1960. The case prompted worldwide press coverage and, with it, an exceptional example of scientific crime detection.

Basil and Freda Thorne, who lived in Bondi, Sydney, made headlines when they won a large New South Wales lottery prize. But their joy was shattered when, on 7 July, their son, Graeme, failed to return home after school. He was quickly reported missing and detectives were at the family home when a man telephoned saying, "I have got your son", and demanded £A25,000 in ransom money.

Every available resource was mustered to find the missing boy and appeals were made in the press and broadcast media for information. Then came a second telephone call from the kidnapper to discuss handing over the ransom. He rang off before his call could be traced. On 16 August, children playing in the north Sydney suburb of Seaforth, discovered Graeme's body. His feet were tied together and he had been strangled with a scarf.

The body was minutely examined for trace evidence and the presence on his clothes of a pink coloured dust suggested he had lain somewhere else before being abandoned in Seaforth. The coloured dust was identified as a type of mortar used in the building trade, suggesting the dead boy might have been stored in a cellar or garage with unrendered walls. An important discovery was mould adhering to the dead boy's shoes. Four different types of fungi were identified of which the most significant was *Aspergillus repens*. This particular mould had a growth pattern which helped to determine the likely time of death. The thinking was that, as the mould favoured a humid atmosphere and undisturbed conditions, the body had probably lain where it was found for about five weeks.

Further examination of the victim's clothing and the rug in which his body had been wrapped, turned up leaf, stem and seed particles which were identified as fragments from two different types of cypress trees, one of which, *Cupressus glabra*, was rare. An expert at the National Herbarium explained that the combination of debris from the two species was very unusual and if a location could be identified where they grew together, that would likely be where the victim was killed.

Faced with the challenge of finding such a location, the police searched entire neighbourhoods around Seaforth. They were equipped with small sprigs of each cypress species so that they knew what to look for. Local knowledge often proves important in police enquiries and, on this occasion, detectives struck gold when they encountered the local postman in the Clontarf district. When they explained their mission, he directed them to a particular house which he thought might be what they were looking for. Situated just over a mile from the spot where Graeme Thorne's body was found was a house in the garden of which stood two cypress trees. As soon as they checked the foliage, investigators knew they had reached their goal and this was confirmed when the garage on the site proved to have been built using distinctive pink mortar.

When police officers knocked on the door, the startled occupant of the house said they had only recently moved in and that the previous tenant, Stephen Leslie Bradley, had left on 7 July, the day Graeme Thorne was kidnapped. When officers learned that Bradley had left Australia on the liner, *Himalaya*, bound for Europe, they issued a warrant for his arrest and he was taken into custody at the ship's first port of call, Colombo in Sri Lanka.

Once returned to Australia, Bradley was tried for kidnap and murder amid an atmosphere of great public hostility. The most sensational crime in Australian history ended with Stephen Bradley's conviction and sentencing to penal servitude for life.

The case was a triumph for the Australian police and scientists who worked together on the investigation. After public reaction had subsided, Detective Sergeant F.B. Cocks of the South Australian Police published an article in *The Australian Police Journal*. Its title was "Taxonomy and Plant Ecology in the Field of Forensic Science". The author placed special emphasis on the importance of botanical evidence.

PUSHING UP THE DAISIES: FORENSIC BOTANY

Luxuriant plant growth is sometimes a marker for searchers looking for a missing body. A patch of disturbed soil will encourage plants and weeds to flourish in ways that capture attention. American botanists have developed methods of determining time of death, or post mortem interval, by studying plants associated with a burial site and comparing their growth with that of established plants of the same species in the surrounding locale.

Unusually lush growth of plants can, therefore, signal something sinister. Such was the case when detectives investigated a fire at the home of Abdul Malik in 1963. Otherwise known as Michael X, he lived in a house called "La Chance" near Port of Spain, Trinidad. His real name was Michael de Freitas. He preached extreme radicalism and engaged in armed robbery and other crimes while presiding over a commune of devotees.

In the wake of the fire, Malik absconded, leaving a wrecked house behind and no sign of his followers. It was while searching the grounds that an astute detective noticed a patch of lettuces which seemed uncommonly "tall and yellow". When the ground was dug up, the body revealed was of Joe Skerritt, one of Malik's henchmen and, nearby, another grave containing the body of a young woman.

Malik was eventually located in Guyana and brought back to Trinidad to face justice. It emerged that Skerritt had been executed for daring to challenge Malik's instructions and his body thrown into a trench. Malik ordered his gardener "to plant a tree" which was the accepted underworld code for using vegetation to cover a gravesite. In this instance, the gardener planted a bed of lettuce, nourished by human compost, which, in due course, told its own story, bearing out the old adage of the "dead pushing up the daisies".

Devotees of crime mysteries will know that forensic investigators routinely examine beneath the fingernails of murder victims and suspects and scrape out what is politely known as subungual debris. Fingernails are consistent collectors of grime from human activities and, as such, can reveal a wealth of information.

Other repositories of debris are noses and ears. Pollen grains, for example, abound in leafy environments of both town and country and, once airborne, as any sufferer of hay fever will experience, may get up your nose. Pollens can be readily identified under a microscope and provide information confirming the presence of a suspect at a particular location. And, like all plant matter, there is a seasonal dimension which can help to define timescales in crime investigations.

Richard Szibor, a German forensic biologist, made a speciality in the 1950s of matching pollen grains found on a suspect's clothing or body to a particular place. He was quoted as saying that pollens are virtually indestructible and may persist in the nasal passages, for example, long after death.

Another part of the body with a reputation as a repository for life's passing grime particles is the ear. This was remarked on by Dr. Edmond **Locard**, the great motivator for examining trace evidence in all its varied forms. In the same way that an individual's craft or calling could be determined by the presence of calluses on his hands, so it was possible to glean the same information from debris retrieved from the ears.

Thus, a building worker would acquire brick dust and a sawmill worker, sawdust in the ears as evidence of their particular labours. Despite high standards of personal cleanliness, these occupational deposits might persist, embedded in earwax, for months. Locard reckoned that in ninety percent of instances, he could discern the occupation of manual workers by looking into their ears.

He recorded his participation in a murder investigation in France when the body of a mushroom grower was found in a ditch some distance from his farm. The grower had been stabbed and his body dragged away across muddy fields where it was dumped. Not surprisingly, in view of his occupation, mushroom spores were found under his fingernails. Once identified in the laboratory, the spores proved to be from a rare type of fungus.

Police rounded up a number of suspects, including a tramp who, it turned out, had a criminal record. The man denied any involvement in the death of the grower, but it was noticed that he was wearing new clothes. Examination of his clothing proved negative for any meaningful trace evidence. But, then Dr. Locard decided to examine the man's ears and removed a sample of cerumen or earwax.

Among a variety of dust particles, the forensic expert found mushroom spores which were a microscopic match for the rare fungus cultivated by the dead grower. Now the chief suspect in a murder case, the tramp admitted killing the grower and dragging his body a long way across fields to put distance between the crime scene and the discovery of the victim. He was duly convicted of murder.

Dr. Hamish **Walls**, a former Director of the Metropolitan Police Laboratory and a skilled practitioner of forensic botany, noted a case which neatly illustrated the power of trace evidence. Called on to examine the body of a girl who had been raped and strangled, he noted the presence of small wood chippings on her clothes. Viewing a sample under the microscope he was able to identify the source as a species of pinewood called *Pinus radiata*.

The chief crime suspect was a butcher's assistant whose workplace was visited by Dr. Walls. In an age when the floors of butchers' shops were strewn with sawdust to soak up blood and bits of stray meat, he noted the presence of tiny fragments which had been chipped off the pinewood block. On examination they proved to be of *Pinus radiata*. Once again forensic botany demonstrated its importance as a tool in the service of crime investigation.

IT'S ALL IN THE MIND

Forensic Psychiatry

Forensic psychiatry is the application of measured understanding to the mental status of individuals who commit criminal acts. The idea that an insane person who lacks understanding of their own actions, or responsibility for them, should be protected from the harshest penalties of the law, has a long history.

The concept of *Mens Rea*, guilty mind, goes back several centuries and was used as the central consideration in judging criminal responsibility. The construction of a crime was that *Mens Rea* was followed by *Actus Rea*, a criminal act; intention was thereby turned into commitment.

Defining what constitutes legal insanity so that courts might judge which mental states or disorders absolved a person from liability and punishment proved difficult to formulate. A landmark case was that involving Daniel M'Naghten who, in 1843, shot and killed the Prime Minister's secretary, Edward Drummond.

M'Naghten who, supposedly, nursed a grievance against the Prime Minister, found himself in the dock at The Old Bailey charged with murder. The court's judgement, having considered the circumstances, was that the defendant was insane and he was duly acquitted. This decision produced a considerable reaction and senior judges were called to account.

The result was a formula known as the M'Naghten Rules, which became established as the acid test for criminal responsibility. The

Rules stated that to put forward a defence of insanity, it was necessary to show that, at the time the act was committed, the accused person was labouring under a defect of reason, from disease of the mind, with the result that he did not understand his actions or realise that what he was doing was wrong. The M'Naghten Rules remained as the litmus test for criminal insanity for over a hundred years.

As psychiatry became a more potent discipline bringing greater insights into the workings of the mind, so the M'Naghten Rules came to be seen as too rigid. This growth in perception led to numerous attempts in Britain and the USA to devise new tests for insanity. One result was the emergence of the concept of irresistible impulse in the USA in 1954. Known as the Durham Rule, it exempted a person from criminal responsibility if it could be shown they had acted under the influence of mental disease or defectiveness.

The Durham Rule was fine-tuned in 1962 with new thinking incorporated in the Model Penal Code. This was based on tests to determine whether a defendant suffered from a lack of capacity either to understand the criminality of his actions or to conform his conduct to the requirements of the law. This had the effect of adding irresistible impulse to the criteria, using a refinement of language which stated that a person may be judged innocent by reason of insanity if they were unable to control their acts even though they knew they were wrong.

The debate on both sides of the Atlantic had become mired in the intricacies of language and there was a feeling that, while psychiatrists used one terminology, the legal system employed a different one. In England, the 1957 Homicide Act permitted pleas of diminished responsibility which placed a new emphasis on mental capacity in a move away from definitions of sanity.

While legal minds were grappling with the nuances of court procedures, forensic psychiatrists were firming up their definitions of the mentally afflicted. Thus, in 1957, Dr. W. Lindesay **Neustatter**, a psychiatrist practising in London, had made a study of contemporary convicted murderers and put them into descriptive categories. He published his work under the title, *The Mind of the Murderer*, and introduced examples of schizophrenia, sadism, paranoia, hysteria and other mental conditions.

A change of emphasis occurred in 1982 when a headline crime

case in the USA resulted in an acquittal which provoked a strong public reaction. In the previous year, twenty-seven year old John Hinckley Jr shot and wounded President Ronald Reagan and injured three others outside the Washington Hilton Hotel.

What was referred to as "the defence of last resort: insanity" was pleaded by Hinckley when he came to court. The onus was on him to prove that he had suffered mental illness so severe that he "lacked substantial capacity to appreciate the wrongfulness of his acts and could no longer control his own conduct".

When the trial verdict of "not guilty by reason of insanity" was announced in June 1982, there was an immediate response from the American public. The verdict had a bearing on deeply felt attitudes regarding crime and punishment. Views were expressed that the insanity defence itself was on trial and questions were asked about whether it should be abolished. Donald Regan, Treasury Secretary at the time, described the verdict as "absolutely atrocious", adding that it was a licence for the "crazies of the world".

Respected journals, such as *The New York Times* and *Newsweek* carried extended coverage arguing the pros and cons of the insanity plea. This high profile case with its definitions and terminology of offenders and their mental capacity put pressure on psychiatry as well as other forensic disciplines.

For centuries, those who committed murder tended to be categorised by motive; for example, gain, revenge and elimination. The view was, that once a motive became lodged in the mind, it evolved into *Mens Rea*, guilty intent. All that remained was for the intending perpetrator to establish a method and create an opportunity in order to fulfil his plan. The idea that action might result from uncontrolled activity of the brain – an irreversible impulse – was a much later notion.

Such an impulse might have applied to Dr. Thomas Neill Cream, found guilty in 1892 of fatally poisoning four women in London. He had a criminal history involving arson, blackmail, abortion and murder. Cream had suffered from extreme short-sightedness since childhood which led to severe headaches, insomnia and drug-taking. In a letter to *The Times*, Cream's optician suggested that the murderer's moral degeneracy might have been attributed to his eye defect with the stigma of being cross-eyed, which he had suffered all his life.

The belief that criminality could be determined by outward physical signs – Lombroso's born criminal – was discredited long before the new discipline of neurocriminology appeared on the scene. A new generation of researchers located significant reduction in the development of the prefrontal cortex in scans made of murderers' brains. This is the part of the brain which controls what is called "executive function" and determines a person's ability to cope with angry and violent impulses.

This was a move away from the search for social and environmental causes of criminal behaviour and focussed instead on the inner sanctum of the brain itself. Professor Adrian Raine at the University of Philadelphia led a team carrying out research into the biological roots of criminality. They put neuroscience on the map with the publication in 2013 of Professor Raine's book, *The Anatomy of Violence: The Biological Roots of Crime*.

Technological advances which made possible sophisticated brain scanning not only opened up new realms of forensic understanding but also provided the legal community with opportunities which they were quick to embrace. Lawyers in the USA developed defence strategies deploying brain scans which indicated the presence of cerebral abnormalities. It could be argued that demonstrable evidence of mental impairment was a basis for reducing criminal intent and, therefore, an argument which should be taken into consideration in the sentencing process. This defence concept became known as, "my brain made me do it".

Unsurprisingly, worries were expressed by the judiciary along the lines that this development would encourage a culture in which criminals could be excused their violent activities on the grounds that they were individuals with demonstrable mental health problems. As the new thinking developed, offering defence lawyers fresh approaches, "neurolaw" cases began to increase, particularly in the USA. In a Florida murder trial in 2010, a man accused of killing his wife avoided the death penalty after brain scans were used in his defence. These indicated abnormality in the frontal lobe of his brain which, it was successfully argued, accounted for his violent behaviour.

Researchers at Duke University in the USA extended the new

thinking with their studies into epigenetics. This is a way of considering how environmental considerations exert an influence on an individual's genetic code. While agreeing that genetic make-up is affected by variations in nature and nurture, scientists ruled out the idea of a "crime gene". Critics of developments in neurocriminology express concerns that the environment is seen as regulating an individual's genetic code to the point where crime is explained away as illness.

Attempts to identify the footprint of criminality seem to have come full circle. From the descriptions of physical anomalies associated with law-breaking behaviour, described by Lombroso and Gall, to the inner sanctum of the brain itself and the secrets of the human genetic code.

Forensic psychiatry has made great advances and understanding of the human mind has been re-mapped. But, there are no absolutes in the search for the seed of criminality, although there are many sign posts along the way.

PART TWO : BIOGRAPHIES

AMOËDO, Dr. Oscar (1863-1945)

Cuban-born Professor of Dentistry working in Paris in the 1890s. He is regarded as the founder of forensic odontology, a branch of forensic medicine which deals with legal procedures for handling dental evidence.

It has been known since Roman times that an individual's teeth can provide vital clues aiding identification. Next to fingerprints and DNA, the teeth are a most reliable indicator of identity. They are remarkably durable and can withstand the passage of time as well as extreme conditions, such as burning and destruction of the body.

Dr. Amoëdo played a major role in identifying victims of the blaze at the Bazar de la Charité Ball in Paris when a cinema projector malfunctioned, causing a disastrous fire in 1897. One hundred and twenty-six people died, of whom, all but thirty were identified odontologically by Amoëdo and his colleagues.

This incident underlined the importance of a new branch of forensic medicine in helping to identify victims of both natural and man-made disasters, including wars and genocide. Amoëdo published an influential document on the subject in 1898, entitled *L'Art Dentaire en Médecine Légale*.

Since his time, forensic odontology has become a more exact science using DNA and state-of-the-art analysis to determine the age, sex and racial origins of human remains. This has particular significance in crime scene investigations where there are multiple victims and also in sex-related crimes where bite marks are a feature.

A FORENSIC FORUM

BALTHAZARD, Professor Victor (1872-1950)
One of the great forensic innovators who graduated from the Ecole Polytechnique in Paris with qualifications in mathematics and technology. A military career beckoned but, after a spell in uniform, he qualified as a doctor and directed his interests towards forensic medicine.

At an early stage in his work as a medical examiner, be focussed on the opportunities provided by trace evidence retrieved from crime scenes. In 1909 he was called on to examine a woman who had been battered to death in her Paris apartment. His attention was drawn to the hands in which were clutched tufts of hair evidently pulled from her attacker's head in a struggle.

That hair might afford important trace evidence in a crime scene investigation had been known since the time of **Orfila**. Balthazard examined the hair microscopically and was able to clear one of two suspects held by the police. The hair appeared to be that of a woman and he noted that while it matched the head hair of the second suspect for colour and diameter, it did not provide conclusive proof. He also observed that some of the hair was in a clump literally torn out by the roots. When he examined the suspect's head he found a place on the scalp from which the hair had been pulled out. This was clinching proof and a murder charge followed.

Balthazard published his studies on human and animal hair in 1910 in a book which for more than a decade was the chief forensic guide to hair examination. Having been appointed Professor of Forensic Medicine at the Sorbonne, he launched into further ground-breaking studies, this time involving the examination of firearms.

The idea that bullets could be associated by the marks on them with the weapon from which they had been fired had been current for some time and scientists at Leipzig had experimented by rolling bullets on waxed paper to make impressions of the marks on them. This was a step, albeit a small one, in the right direction.

Balthazard was convinced that these marks were vital to the process of identifying bullets. His opportunity to prove his conjecture came, inevitably, with a murder by shooting. With the aid of photographs, he successfully demonstrated that the fatal bullets removed from the victim's body matched test bullets fired from the suspected murder weapon.

In 1912, Professor Balthazard gave a paper on his findings to the Congress of Legal Medicine in Paris. In the following year, he published his conclusions which were a personal triumph and a curtain raiser for the new science of forensic ballistics.

BARR, Dr. Murray Llewellyn (1908-1995)

In 1948 two Canadian scientists, Barr and Ewart George Bertram, observed that the nuclei in the cells of female tissue usually contained a distinctive structure, likened to a drumstick, which was rarely found in males.

This structure, which became known as a Barr body, is most noticeable in white blood cells and the epithelial cells lining the mouth. Their appearance in blood of unknown origin is a basis for identifying it is of female origin.

BASS, Dr. William M. (1928-)

One of America's "bone detectives" who established the Anthropological Research Facility, popularly known as "the body farm", in 1981. He set up an anthropology department at the University of Tennessee in 1971 and was appointed the State's first forensic anthropologist.

His mission was to establish time of death from the condition of a corpse and related environmental factors. To that end, using donated human and animal cadavers, he set up "the body farm" by placing remains in the ground and subjecting them to a variety of disposal conditions in order to measure rates of decay. This enabled environmental factors such as climate, temperature, humidity and insect activity to be gauged. Studying the life cycle of insects as markers of likely time of death was particularly significant.

Dr. Bass referred to bodies as "brimming with data", for, though the flesh is corrupted, the bones survive. They can reveal sex, age, stature and race as well as the effects of disease and injuries, all vital components in establishing the identity of human remains.

In 2004 he published *Death's Acre*, co-written with Jon Jefferson, and his *Human Osteology: A Laboratory and Field Manual*, published in 1971, remains an authoritative text.

BAYLE, Edmond (1879-1929)
Studied physics and chemistry and began his working career at the Pasteur Institute in Paris. In 1915, he applied for a job working with **Bertillon** in the Identification Service and developed an interest in scientific criminology. He was particularly interested in secret writing and ways of revealing it using chemicals. He was made Head of the Identification Service in 1921.

Bayle was quick to learn from his contemporaries elsewhere in Europe, particularly Lyon and Berlin. Spectral analysis of chemical substances led him to apply the method to criminal investigation work. In due course, his researches led to the development of spectrophotometry, a means whereby chemicals such as paint flakes could be identified when found as trace evidence at a crime scene.

In 1924, he succeeded Bertillon as Director of the Laboratory of the Judicial Police in Paris. In the same year, he applied his analytical skills to a case in which a man's body was found dumped in the Bois de Boulogne. The clothing on the corpse revealed traces of sawdust and coal dust which led Bayle to believe the crime had been committed in a cellar and the body subsequently dumped.

Most significant were flakes of red paint found on the dead man's trousers. Police enquiries led them to a bookmaker with whom the victim had gambling links. A search of the cellar at this man's house revealed paint flakes that Bayle matched spectrographically to those found on the victim's clothing. Thus was the linking evidence established and the importance of crime scene evidence emphasised.

Bayle's career ended on a tragic note when, at the age of fifty, he was fatally shot on the steps of the Palais de Justice by a deranged psychopath.

BERTILLON, Alphonse (1853-1914)
French criminologist who used scientific methods to devise a system of criminal identification. This was based on the knowledge that the structure of the human frame remains unchanged throughout life. Therefore, by systematically measuring various parts of the body, a unique profile is created of an individual which is part of his identity.

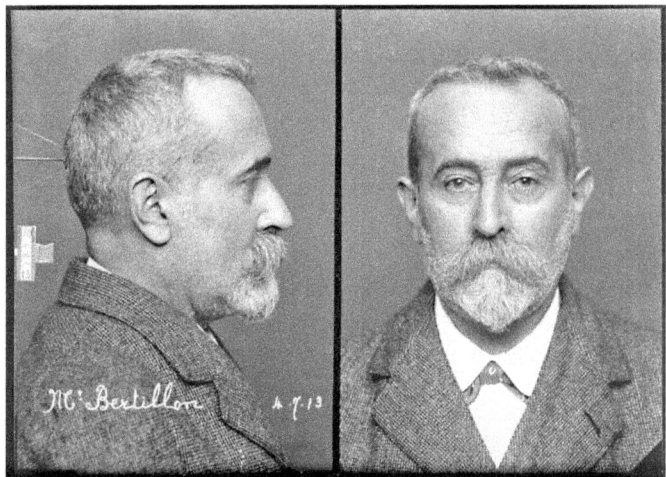

Bertillon called his method, anthropometry, or man measurement, and it is sometimes referred to as Bertillonage. The principle was also shared by Lambert **Quetelet**, the Belgian statistician, who demonstrated that no two individuals have the same measurements.

From his lowly position as a clerk in the Paris Préfecture of Police, Bertillon prepared a report on his methods which he presented to his superiors in 1879. Bertillonage won acceptance as the preferred method of criminal identification in France and, in 1888, Bertillon was appointed Director of the Department of Judicial Identity. The system gained wide acceptance throughout Europe and, after Bertillon successfully identified the murderous bomber, Ravachol, in Paris in 1892, he was treated as a national hero.

Bertillon also pioneered the use of forensic photography and developed the concept of portrait parlé (speaking likeness) as an aid to identification. The method involved photographing an individual's full face and profile. Distinguishing facial features were each given a code letter, thereby enabling a short-hand formula to be used by police forces to exchange information about criminal suspects.

Just as he was reaching the peak of his fame, Bertillon faced a challenge from a rival identification system – fingerprinting – which was destined to supersede anthropometry. He opposed the new methods and refused to include fingerprinting, which amounted to another form of measurement, into his own thinking.

With the dawn of the twentieth century, the fingerprint classification system devised by Sir Edward **Henry**, swept around the world completely eclipsing Bertillonage. Even his great contemporaries, **Locard** and **Lacassagne**, could not persuade Bertillon to accept the significance of fingerprint identification.

Bertillon's health deteriorated and he died an embittered man at the age of sixty-one. He has his rightful place in the forensic hall of fame and, despite the short life of the system he devised, he had demonstrated the value of applying scientific logic to the needs of criminal identification.

BORDET, Dr. Jules
(1870-1961)

While working at the Pasteur Institute in Paris, Bordet made discoveries about the human immune system which provided the foundation for serology, the study of blood fluids. Born in Belgium, he qualified in medicine at Brussels and made a career choice to work as a bacteriologist in Paris carrying out research on immunisation.

In 1895, Bordet identified the antitoxins in blood serum that provided protection against disease. Working in the laboratory with rabbits in search of a vaccine against diphtheria, he found that, in addition to destroying invasive bacteria, the antitoxins also killed off foreign blood cells. Blood serum developed the same defensive reaction during experiments using milk injections. A response was induced whereby the antitoxins attached the protein, which formed a deposit called precipitin.

This was the enabling step which led to the precipitin test, making it possible for the first time to distinguish between human and animal blood. This work was of enormous significance in advancing crime investigation procedures and marked the beginnings of forensic serology.

Dr. Bordet published his work on precipitins in 1899 and other researchers, notably Dr. Paul **Uhlenhuth**, perfected the precipitin test.

BRASH, James Couper (1886-1958)

Professor of Anatomy at the University of Edinburgh who worked with John **Glaister** on the forensic aspects of the Ruxton case in 1935. The discovery of dismembered human remains amounting to seventy pieces, posed a major challenge in victim identification.

Brash and Glaister assembled the remains and partially reconstructed two bodies, using state-of-the-art anatomical and radiographic techniques. Identifying features had been removed from the two heads and, while there were presumed identities, this fell short of proof. The puzzle was resolved by the use of ground breaking methodology.

By superimposing a photograph of Mrs. Ruxton, one of the assumed victims, over an x-ray photograph of one of the skulls, a match was found which showed the correspondence of numerous facial features. The second skull was similarly identified and the deaths of the two women were attributed to Dr. Buck Ruxton. He acknowledged his crimes.

The two professors, Brash and Glaister, wrote a book entitled *Medico-Legal Aspects of the Ruxton Case*. Dr. Brash was widely acknowledged as a leading anatomist and served in several senior academic and teaching posts.

BROUARDEL, Professor Paul Camille Hippolyte (1837-1906)

Forensic specialists in France in the nineteenth century led the way in understanding the evidence of strangling and suffocation on the human body. **Tardieu**'s studies of asphyxial death and interpretation of the resultant tell-tale haemorrhages were timely and significant.

Paul Brouardel, who was appointed professor of forensic medicine in Paris in 1877, made a special study of the behaviour of blood in bodies suspected of having been subjected to fatal violence. He was aware that a favoured method of murderers was first to kill their victim and then hang the body to simulate death by suicide. Brouardel noted that, following death, the blood of a hanged individual coagulated within the first hour and then returned to a liquid state. This inspired his research into the coagulation of blood as an indicator of time of death.

The Parisian forensic science establishment suffered a setback in 1905 in a case which inspired public indignation. This was the trial for murder of Jeanne Weber, accused of asphyxiating three children. Brouardel's finding was that the evidence did not amount to suffocation as proposed by the prosecution and Weber was found not guilty. When, three years later, Weber was charged with further murders and found guilty, public opinion turned against the original experts who, it was claimed, had overlooked signs of strangulation. By this time, Brouardel had died.

He published the results of his studies relating to strangulation and suffocation in 1897 and stressed the role of the expert in court was to avoid speculation and "...bear witness within the limits of science".

BRUSSEL, Dr. James A. (1905-1982)

A psychiatrist in private practice in New York City for nearly fifty years, Brussel's expertise was increasingly called on by law enforcement agencies. He is credited with establishing the first systematic offender profile in a criminal case. The press chose to refer to him as the "Sherlock Holmes of the Couch", a comparison which he declined, except for his pipe-smoking habit which he shared with the great detective.

Dr. Brussel served in the US Army Medical Corps during World War Two and later, in Korea where he headed up centres for neuropsychiatric treatment. This background afforded him unparalleled experience in dealing with disturbed behaviour. When he returned to civilian life, he found he was increasingly called on for guidance by law enforcement agencies.

While psychiatric profiling had been practised for some time in the sphere of military intelligence, it had not been extended to criminal profiling in civilian settings. That changed in 1957 when Brussel was asked by the New York Police Department to help identify the "Mad Bomber", as he was known, who had been terrifying the city for sixteen years.

Since 1940, the bomber had planted sixteen devices in public buildings, telephone booths and theatres. They were not all detonated but those that were caused damage to property and resulted in many injuries although no deaths. A reign of terror was thereby created, heightened by the bomber's taunts in the form of letters sent to the press. When a bomb exploded in a Brooklyn theatre, injuring six people, in 1956, Dr. Brussel was called in.

On the basis of information provided by the NYPD, he compiled a detailed profile of the bomber. He suggested that the letters denoted an individual who planned ahead. Someone who had been a model employee with a better than average education, probably of Slavic origin and living in Connecticut. He was a loner, living with an elderly relative and a person who craved attention. To the astonishment of the police, Brussel added that when the bomber was found, he would be wearing a buttoned-up, double-breasted suit.

The profile was released to the press and resulted in a tentative identification of George Metesky drawn from the files of his former employer. When confronted, Metesky readily confessed and appeared in a buttoned-up suit to be taken into police custody. He was judged to be insane and, for his part, Brussel commented that his contribution to the outcome was a blend of "science, intuition and hope".

In his book, *Casebook of a Crime Psychiatrist*, published in 1968, Brussel wrote that his aim was to study a person's deeds and thereby deduce what kind of individual might have carried them out. He noted that if a psychiatrist was also a criminologist, "he simply wanted to know the reasons for all human reactions to life's stimuli". Thus was offender profiling put on the map.

BURRARD, Major Sir Gerald (1888-1965)

Decorated former artillery officer during World War One who became a leading expert on firearms, particularly shotguns. He wrote extensively as a gun correspondent for leading publications such as *The Field* and in 1934 published a comprehensive work with the title, *The Identification of Firearms and Forensic Ballistics*. This was written to meet the needs for a guide which dealt with the fundamentals of firearms, particularly related to issues arising in the courts. He also addressed members of the Medico-legal Society on the subject of forensic ballistics, introducing them to an emerging new science.

He made a comprehensive study of the microscopic examination of fired bullets and cartridges. It was in this domain that he first crossed swords with Robert **Churchill** in 1925 and there was a further clash in 1932. Burrard was considered a foremost authority on shotguns and Churchill, with his short-barrelled shotgun, invaded the territory of the author of *The Modern Shotgun*.

Described as "one of the greatest living experts on firearms", Burrard gave evidence at numerous criminal trials, frequently in opposition to Churchill. Describing his methods, he wrote, "I have accepted no result which I have not checked, re-checked and checked again". His work represented a milestone in the development of firearms' examination.

BYRNES, Thomas F. (1842-1910)

Legendary New York detective who courted controversy while demonstrating his talent for organisation. Byrnes was born in Ireland, fought in the American Civil War and joined the NYPD in 1863.

He was quickly promoted to captain of police and made head of the New York Detective Bureau. He resolved to end corrupt practices which had allowed police and gangland to co-exist. In 1880, he established a well trained and organised detective force comprising forty officers.

Byrnes soon became America's most talked about police officer, boasting of the convictions he had secured and the total of jail time served in consequence. He also set up a museum at police headquarters where he displayed various crime artefacts with the intention of intimidating prisoners under interrogation.

Fingerprinting was slow to gain recognition in the USA but, realising the need for a criminal identification system, Byrnes began a practice of photographing every criminal that came under his jurisdiction. His "rogues gallery" was published in book form in 1886 as *Professional Criminals of America*. It contained descriptions as well as photographs of over two hundred individuals some of whom had colourful aliases such as "Banjo Pete" and "Oyster Jim". Byrnes's initiative had resonance with the use of photography pioneered by **Bertillon** in Europe as part of a system of identification.

His career ended on a controversial note in 1895 when he failed to gain re-appointment as Chief of Police on the grounds that he was unable to explain how he had acquired his considerable wealth which some believed was due to malpractice.

CAMERON, Professor James Malcolm (1930-2003)

Pathologist and pioneer of forensic dentistry. In 1973, he succeeded Francis **Camps** as professor of forensic medicine at London Hospital Medical College and, in 1978 was appointed President of the British Academy of Forensic Sciences. He also edited the journal, *Medicine, Science and Law*.

With B.G. Sims as co-author, he published *Forensic Dentistry* in 1973. This was a landmark publication following Scandinavian pre-eminence in this field led by Professor **Gustafson**.

Professor Cameron gave evidence at the Dingo Baby trial in Australia in a high profile and controversial murder case. In August

1980, a nine-week old baby disappeared from her parents' tent during a camping holiday near Ayers Rock. Michael and Lindy Chamberlain and their three children were preparing for bed when Lindy claimed to have seen a dingo (wild dog) in the half darkness. When she checked the baby's cot, it was empty. "The dingo's got my baby," she exclaimed.

In due course, a coroner's inquest ruled that the infant had indeed been killed by a dingo. The body was never found but a bloodstained jumpsuit and vest were recovered. Following a review of the evidence, Lindy Chamberlain was tried for murder. Professor Cameron's appraisal of the evidence was that there was nothing to support the dingo theory while an examination of the baby's clothing suggested she had her throat cut. The jury delivered a guilty verdict.

CAMPS, Professor F.E. (1905-1972)

A graduate of Guy's Hospital Medical School, he decided to specialise in forensic medicine and followed a career which established him as one of the leading pathologists of his time. He built up the forensic department at London Hospital Medical School where he lectured and was appointed professor in 1963.

He was involved in many headline murder investigations and developed a bold approach to his work. He had an inclination for experimentation and reconstruction in crime investigation. In 1955, he was called on to carry out a post mortem examination on the body of a British soldier serving in Germany who, ostensibly, had committed suicide by hanging himself. Doubts had arisen over the verdict reached by a military court when it was learned that the dead man had been involved in a dispute with another NCO.

Camps concluded from his examination of the exhumed body that the hanging had been contrived to cover up the real cause of death which was a blow to the throat that had fractured the thyroid cartilage. The pathologist believed the fatal injury had been due to a Karate chop. He staged a reconstruction of the crime and arranged for a Japanese ju-jitsu expert to demonstrate how such a blow might be delivered. Camps was confident that a commando-style chop had resulted in the death. It was, he said, a matter of "straightforward mechanics". A court martial was held and Sergeant

Frederick Emmett-Dunne was held to have killed his fellow soldier with a single blow and then staged a fake suicide.

Dr. Camps visited the USA where he established a professional working relationship with Dr. **Gradwohl** in St. Louis. Influenced by the American pathologist, **Camps** set up the British Academy of Forensic Sciences in 1958 and became its President. During this period, he edited the journal, *Medicine, Science and the Law*, an important publication which brought three professions together. He also edited **Gradwohl**'s book, *Legal Medicine*, for which he was awarded the Swiney Prize in 1969.

CANTER, Professor David (1944-)

David Canter developed a new discipline of investigative psychology which focussed on offender profiling and criminal mapping. While heading the Department of Psychology at the University of Surrey in 1986, he created an offender profile which helped the police to capture a serial rapist and murderer. This was the first occasion this procedure had been used in Britain.

During the course of analysing reports of a series of sex attacks which had taken place in London over a four-year period, he perceived a pattern and alerted the police to his findings. Crime investigators asked Canter to draw up an offender profile of the so-called "Railway Rapist".

Working from witnesses' descriptions and using his knowledge of criminal psychology, he devised a profile of a man, defining his age, height, personality as a loner and history of his sexual crimes. He added that the man was a careful planner who worked in a semi-skilled job. Crucially, Professor Canter noted the spread of crime locations and calculated their epicentre. He determined that the "Railway Rapist's" comfort zone was in the Kilburn area of north London.

Using this information, investigators looked at their files of known sex offenders in the area and came up with the name of John Francis Duffy who they placed under surveillance. He had a history of sexual offences, had worked as a carpenter on the rail network and lived in Kilburn. In due course, Duffy was tried and convicted of five rapes and two murders. Professor Canter's profile had proved remarkably accurate.

Canter went on to set up the Centre for Investigative Psychology at the University of Liverpool in 1994 and, later, was appointed Professor of Psychology at Huddersfield University. He has assisted law enforcement agencies around the world and contributes to the academic literature of his subject. He published *Criminal Shadows* in 1994 and *Mapping Murder* in 2003.

Of his work on criminal mapping he noted that "criminals write their own stories", while, "psychology may help to read them".

CASPER, Johann Ludwig (1796-1864)

The time he spent working in the mortuaries of Berlin inspired him to seek better conditions and working protocols. Forensic medicine at the time was regarded as hack-work by more fashionable doctors and, consequently, training and resources were scarce. Mortuaries were noted for being ill-lit, poorly ventilated and lacking in hygiene.

Methods for carrying out autopsies were often crude with needless damage inflicted on corpses and organs hastily disposed of without proper examination. Even as late as the 1890s, **Lacassagne** felt obliged to criticise the careless post mortem work carried out by many doctors.

Casper made it his mission to improve forensic practices in Berlin and, as his influence grew, so his methods were more widely adopted. In 1850, he published *Forensic Dissection*, a book which became a standard text. He stressed the importance of rigorous examination and careful observation backed-up by microscopic and chemical scrutiny of body tissues.

He was appointed Director of the Institute of Legal Medicine in Berlin in 1850 and, six years later, distilled his experience into a classic publication, *The Practical Manual of Forensic Medicine*, which set out protocols to guide the development of this branch of medicine.

CHRISTISON, Sir Robert (1797-1882)

Nineteenth-century toxicologist who qualified in medicine at Edinburgh in 1819 and went to Paris to study under the great

forensic pioneer, Mathieu **Orfila**. He returned to Edinburgh as Professor of Medical Jurisprudence.

He was a witness at many celebrated murder trials, including that of Madeleine Smith, accused in 1857 of poisoning her paramour with arsenic. Christison was questioned about the feasibility of disguising arsenic by administering it in chocolate or cocoa drinks. He said he had tasted arsenic which he found slightly sweet but undetectable in cocoa or coffee. The trial jury brought in a Scottish verdict of Not Proven.

Christison noted that, "...although the most skilful have tried to define a poison, everyone has hitherto failed". While he made his name as a toxicologist who was not afraid to experiment, some of his other work was less well known. In particular, he made a study of the pathology of the kidneys and contributed to the understanding of nephrology.

His adventurous approach to poisons was exemplified by the famous account made in 1855 of the occasion when he dosed himself with Calabar bean. The so-called 'ordeal bean' was used in West Africa to test people suspected of practising witchcraft or other crimes. If the suspect survived consumption of the bean, their innocence was proven. Christison survived the ordeal.

A medical use was found for the bean when it was discovered that its active component, physostigmine, could be used to contract the pupil of the eye.

CHURCHILL, Robert (1886-1958)

Gun maker who helped to pioneer firearms examination in Britain, making particular use of the comparison microscope. Building on the work of Calvin **Goddard** in the USA and Sir Sydney

Smith, he developed his skills as a ballistics specialist.

In 1912, he testified at the trial of John Williams who was charged with using a revolver to shoot and kill a police officer. Churchill successfully matched the fatal bullet to the weapon that fired it and supported his evidence in court by using photographs to prove his case. It was the first occasion in Britain that a projectile was matched to a specific weapon.

He went on to compile a catalogue of the rifling characteristics inside the barrel of every known make of revolver and automatic pistol available in Britain at the time. This was an echo of a similar task carried out in the USA by his contemporary Charles **Waite**.

As his expertise became more widely known, Churchill was called on to give evidence in cases involving firearms, including that of Browne and Kennedy in 1927. Following publicity about the trial, George Bernard Shaw in a letter to *The Daily News* dismissed ballistics evidence on the grounds that it was nothing more than coincidences. Churchill gave a vigorous response, asserting that "no two weapons have the same mark", adding that it was impossible to fake marks which were only visible under a microscope.

With the advent of World War Two, Churchill's contribution was to train service personnel in the handling of weapons. This included the Home Guard who were advised to "shoot on the wing" at German parachutists descending out of the skies over Britain.

Robert Churchill's life and contribution to firearms examination was recorded by Macdonald Hastings in his book, *The Other Mr Churchill*, published in 1963.

COOMBS, Dr. Robin (1921-2006)

Cambridge scientist whose method for detecting rhesus antibodies represented a major breakthrough in immunology. The Rhesus factor in blood typing had been discovered by Karl **Landsteiner** in 1940. Coombs unravelled the process and devised a sensitive test whereby rhesus antibodies could be detected.

The significance of this development was that it added another dimension to existing blood grouping characteristics which helped the process of identifying individuals involved in criminal investigations.

The frontiers of serology were thereby pushed forward and blood grouping gained in importance. The aim was to define a unique blood code for every human being – a kind of blood fingerprint. The eventual discovery of DNA would turn this into reality.

Working with a team of serologists, Coombs developed a sensitive method enabling small amounts of blood residue to be grouped with greater accuracy. Dr. Coombs served as professor at Cambridge University for twenty-five years and was elected a fellow of The Royal Society in 1965.

DOYLE, Sir Arthur Conan (1859-1930)

Famed creator of the fictional detective, Sherlock Holmes, and a campaigner for justice. Doyle qualified as a doctor at Edinburgh and, during the period 1882 to 1890, worked as a general practitioner. He then changed career and turned to his writing skills. In 1886 he published *A Study in Scarlet* and Sherlock Holmes was born.

Doyle was a contemporary of some of the great forensic pioneers in Europe such as **Bertillon**, **Gross** and **Locard**. They learned from each other and laid the foundations for a scientific approach to criminology. When Holmes made his appearance, the great detective was frequently pictured in his laboratory testing and analysing crime materials.

Apart from his output of Holmes stories, Doyle also involved himself with crime in the real world and, notably, two miscarriages of justice which he helped to rectify. In 1903 George Edalji, a Staffordshire solicitor, was convicted on charges of mutilating farm animals. Doyle investigated the background to the charges and showed that the evidence against Edalji was spurious. Thanks to his intervention, the accused man who had been judged guilty was given a pardon in 1907.

Another miscarriage of justice that Doyle helped to rectify concerned Oscar Slater who, in 1909, was convicted of murdering an elderly woman in Glasgow. He was sentenced to death but secured a reprieve, serving eighteen years in prison. Doyle, helped by famed crime historian William Roughead, showed the flaws in the case made against Slater, particularly inconsistent police testimony, and evidence that the real murderers had been protected from prosecution.

Doyle published *The Case of Oscar Slater* in 1912 and attended the successful appeal sixteen years later when the original judgement was set aside. Doyle became an early member of The Crimes Club, an exclusive gathering of professionals with an interest in criminology. He gave lectures to club members on both the Edalji and Slater cases.

The emphasis placed on trace evidence by Sherlock Holmes owed everything to Doyle's imagination and drew fiction and reality together. He saw the evidential value of contact traces transferred to a criminal from a crime scene. Everything from tobacco ash on clothing and mud on shoes was scrutinised. Where Doyle led, others followed and crime scene investigation took a great leap forward.

Always busy with his pen, Doyle wrote several historical novels and became a follower of spiritualism and lectured on subjects such as crime and clairvoyance. He retired to his home in Sussex where he continued to write until his death at the age of seventy-one.

DWIGHT, Dr. Thomas (1843-1911)

Regarded as the father of American developments in forensic anthropology, the study of the physical structure of the human body. He was Professor of Anatomy at Harvard University where he pioneered techniques for identifying skeletons in terms of their sex, age and height.

Dr. Dwight's paper on this subject, delivered in 1878, was the first formal presentation of its kind and set out the guidelines of forensic anthropology and its development in the USA. The new methodology was destined to play an increasingly important part in the modern world as forensic investigators sought to identify the remains of long dead victims of wars, genocide, natural disasters and murder.

One of Dwight's students was Dr. George Dorsey who came to prominence in the investigation of a murder in Chicago in 1897. Sausage maker, Adolph Luetgert, was suspected as having murdered his wife and disposing of her body. A search of the basement at his sausage factory, centred on the contents of a vat containing a potash mixture.

Sifting through the contents of the vat, investigators found four bone fragments which Luetgert claimed were of animal origin. Dr. Dorsey was called in to examine the small fragments and he determined that they were human and female. His conclusion was supported by the discovery of Mrs. Luetgert's wedding ring in the vat.

Despite the strength of the evidence, Luetgert's first trial ended in stalemate and a hung jury. A second trial, though, provided a platform for Dr. Dorsey who proved to the jury's satisfaction that the bone fragments were part of a human female skeleton. His contribution as an expert witness, the first occasion when an anthropologist was called to give evidence, was acknowledged as masterly. Adolph Luetgert was judged guilty of murder and forensic anthropology gained wide recognition.

DUNCAN, Dr. Andrew
(1744-1828)

Known as Duncan the elder, on account of the fact that his son, also named Andrew, followed a medical career and became the first professor of medical jurisprudence at Edinburgh University.

Duncan the elder was a pioneering doctor and communicator. In 1773, he began publishing a quarterly journal of medicine aimed at keeping practitioners up to date on developments in the profession. He also founded a free hospital in Edinburgh and was appointed Professor of Medicine.

He delivered the first formal lecture on forensic medicine in Britain at Edinburgh University in 1801. Another notable first was the professorship in the new discipline awarded to Dr. Duncan's son in 1807.

Duncan was honoured in his lifetime with many appointments.

EBER, Dr. Wilhelm

German veterinarian working in Berlin in the late 1880s, who made observations about the possibility of using fingerprints for identification purposes. His experience working in the city's abattoirs acquainted him with the practice whereby slaughtermen wiped their hands on towels and left behind bloody imprints.

By studying these impressions, Eber noticed papillary lines on the hands and fingers. After careful observation, he became convinced that each handprint was recognisably different. Pursuing his interest he discovered that he could identify individual slaughtermen by their handprints.

Like Henry **Faulds**, he saw the potential that fingerprints offered for personal identification. In 1888, he approached the Prussian Ministry of the Interior, hoping to initiate a discussion on his discovery. Disappointingly, his approach was spurned and, like Faulds, he suffered disappointment and rejection of his ideas.

Eber persisted with his study of fingerprints and made several innovations. One of these was the use of fuming iodine to develop and preserve latent fingerprints on paper surfaces. Wilhelm Eber is one of the forgotten pioneers of fingerprint examination.

ECKERT, Dr. William G. (1926-1999)

A forensic pathologist with an international reputation for successfully investigating suspicious and violent deaths. He graduated in history from New York University and served in both the US army and navy during World War Two. Following military service, he qualified in medicine and worked as a medical examiner and coroner.

In 1968, he was consulted by Dr. Thomas Noguchi, the coroner who conducted the inquest into the shooting of Senator Robert Kennedy. Two years earlier, Eckert had been instrumental in setting up the International Reference Organisation in Forensic Medicine (INFORM) with the aim of providing a source of expertise for forensic pathologists throughout the USA. The particular concern in the aftermath of Robert Kennedy's death was to avoid the controversy which had surrounded the post mortem of his brother, the late President, in 1963.

Dr. Eckert was a unifier and did much to enhance the standing of forensic medicine. He founded the *Journal of Forensic Medicine and Pathology* and, in 1975, set up the International Institute of Forensic Medicine and Sciences at Wichita, Kansas. His interest in history took him down some unusual paths. In the 1980s he attempted to apply offender profiling methods to the long unsolved murders committed by Jack the Ripper in London a century earlier.

In 1985, he travelled to Brazil as a member of an international team to examine the remains thought to be those of Josef Mengele, the infamous doctor of the Nazi death camp at Auschwitz. DNA samples provided by family members enabled examiners to confirm that the remains of the man drowned in 1979 were those of Doctor Mengele.

In 1962, Dr. Eckert named the institution he had established in Wichita as the Milton Helpern International Center for the Forensic Sciences. In this way he honoured the memory of Dr. Milton **Helpern**, the renowned Chief Medical Examiner of New York City. The center houses a national collection of books and documents relating to legal medicine which was the first of its kind in the USA.

ERZINCLIOGLU, Dr. Zakaria (1951-2002)

Forensic entomology has a long history, although it has only come into prominence since the 1960s. Dr. Erzinclioglu, a man of Turkish origins known to his associates as "Zak", was fascinated by insects since childhood. He inherited an enquiring mind from his father who was a pathologist, and graduated in England as a zoologist. For his doctoral thesis he chose to study blowflies and the way they spread disease.

Insect life provides vital clues in helping to establish time of death. The interaction between insects and dead bodies, involving the growth of maggots and development through their life cycle, provides a reliable indicator of when death occurred. This is especially helpful in missing person's investigations.

Dr. Erzinclioglu assisted the police in 1989 when unidentified remains were found in Cardiff. By examining entomological evidence on the body and its surroundings, he calculated that the person had been in the ground for at least five years. This put the year of death in 1984 and police identified the remains as those of a girl who went missing three years earlier.

In another case, he used maggot evidence on a body to pinpoint the day on which the subject had died. His interpretation of crime scene evidence helped to bring about a successful prosecution. Detectives jokingly referred to Doctor "Zac" as their "maggotologist".

Dr. Erzinclioglu published widely and, while working at Cambridge University, was regularly called on by the Home Office to help in murder investigations. In 1994, he was appointed Director of the Forensic Science Research Centre at Durham. He was a strong advocate of the need for independence in forensic practice. In 2000, he published *Forensics*, a book on crime scene investigation.

FAULDS, Dr. Henry (1843-1930)

Scottish surgeon who worked as a medical missionary in Japan in the 1870s. He was aware that it was a Japanese custom to use fingerprints and handprints as signatures and also for decoration purposes. His interest led him to attempt to classify fingerprints with the possibility that prints found at a crime scene could be compared with a suspect's. Working with the Tokyo police, he convincingly demonstrated the innocence of one crime suspect while confirming the guilt of another.

Faulds wrote a letter about his work with fingerprints to the journal *Nature,* which was published in October 1880. His claims triggered off what would prove to be an ongoing and, at times, acrimonious, discussion. William **Herschel**, recently returned from India, wrote a letter to the journal pointing out that he had been working with fingerprints for twenty years. Clearly, he did not wish

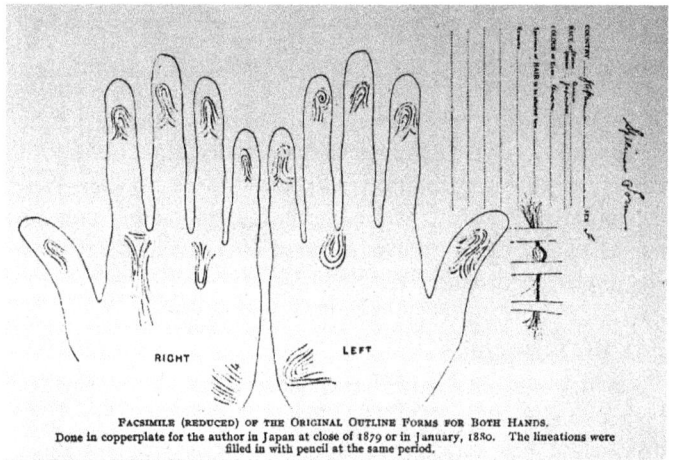

FACSIMILE (REDUCED) OF THE ORIGINAL OUTLINE FORMS FOR BOTH HANDS.
Done in copperplate for the author in Japan at close of 1879 or in January, 1880. The lineations were filled in with pencil at the same period.

to concede any recognition to Dr. Faulds.

Disturbed that, as he saw it, his supremacy in this new field was being usurped, Faulds wrote to many prominent scientists of the day to state his case. He also tried to interest the Home Office in London and the Metropolitan Police in his ideas and asked to be allowed to state his case for fingerprint identification. He was rebuffed at every turn and became embittered about being rejected.

Faulds continued to campaign for acknowledgement but sensed a conspiracy against him, nurtured by Herschel and Francis **Galton**. His worst suspicions were confirmed when Galton published an article in *Nature* in 1891 in which he acknowledged Herschel but ignored Faulds.

He was vindicated, though, in a landmark criminal trial in London in 1905 when two petty criminals were convicted of a double murder on the evidence of a thumbprint left on a cash box. This was the first criminal conviction in England achieved with fingerprint evidence.

Ironically, Faulds advised the defence team at the trial, suggesting that Scotland Yard had been negligent in handling the fingerprint evidence. It was the action of an embittered man against the injustice he believed had been perpetrated against him. While Faulds was treated with disdain, Galton and Herschel received all the accolades for their work on fingerprints which had secured the first criminal conviction of its kind in Britain.

With the passage of time, Dr. Faulds has come to be recognised as the originator of the concept that fingerprints left at a crime scene can be matched to those of a suspect. His genius underwrites the science of fingerprinting and its worldwide acceptance. When the controversy over his failure to gain recognition died down, he moved to Staffordshire where he opted for a less fractious life by working as a police surgeon.

FAUROT, Joseph A. (1872-1942)

America was one of the first countries to follow Britain's lead in adopting a fingerprint identification system. In June 1903, prisoners at New York Sing Sing prison were fingerprinted and, in the following year, a system was installed by the St. Louis Police Department. In 1923 the Federal Fingerprint Bureau was set up.

In 1906, serving as a police lieutenant in New York, Joseph Faurot was despatched to London to learn at firsthand about the newly developed fingerprint classification system. On returning to the USA, he enthusiastically encouraged the adoption of the new method of identification and encouraged police departments to adopt new skills.

Faurot made a breakthrough in 1908 when his methods helped to solve a murder case. His first objective was to eliminate investigating officers' prints, thereby isolating suspect prints. By this means, he reinforced the principle that nothing at a crime scene should be handled or disturbed without due care.

In due course, he established the New York Police Department's Fingerprint Bureau and retired in 1930 with the rank of deputy commissioner.

FIRTH, Dr. James Brierley (1888-1966)

Leading forensic specialist who played a major role in establishing a regional forensic science service in the UK. He spent the early part of his career as a college lecturer and, in 1938, was asked by the Home Office to set up a regional forensic science laboratory for the north west region.

His work encouraged local police forces to consult him on crime investigatory work and, during World War Two, he was seconded to the War Office to work on explosives. After the war ended, he extended his expertise to include fire investigation which, hitherto, had been lacking in the use of scientific methodology.

Firth demonstrated the versatility of forensic science in a wide range of investigations and, in the process, made himself an expert in the examination of hair, textiles, bloodstains and firearms. In 1960, he published a memoir, *A Scientist Turns to Crime*, in which he recorded many of his investigations and noted, "The forensic scientist can often add something of significance to the medical evidence".

The ascendancy of forensic medicine had peaked at this time with the realisation that the way forward was to embrace other scientific disciplines in common purpose. Firth was a strong advocate of this approach and put principle into practice when he returned to the North Western Forensic Science Laboratory as Director. In 2009, a new forensic science teaching facility was opened at Preston and named in honour of J.B. Firth.

FRANKLIN, Dr. Rosalind (1920-1958)

A specialist in the use of X-ray crystallography who learned her skills in Paris at the end of World War Two. In 1951, she became a researcher at King's College working with Maurice Wilkins.

Dr. Franklin is chiefly remembered for some of the wrong reasons in that her contribution to the ground-breaking understanding of the structure of DNA went unrecognised. Her role in the discovery of the double helix was pivotal but others took the credit.

Francis Crick and James Watson, working at Cambridge University, developed a theory about the molecular structure of DNA but lacked the X-ray photographs of DNA crystals which confirmed its structure. The clinching X-ray photograph was provided by Dr. Franklin.

While Crick, Watson and Wilkins were awarded the Nobel Prize in 1962, Franklin received neither award nor commendation. This injustice was belatedly recognised in 2015 and given public prominence by the stage play, *Photograph 51*.

GALL, Dr. Franz Josef (1758-1828)

As a keen observer of his fellow human beings, Gall became absorbed by the possibilities of relating variations in the shape of the human skull to the function of the brain beneath. These were the beginnings of what would come to be called phrenology.

Believing the mind is an assembly of faculties located in the brain, he set out to define them and relate their function to different aspects of human behaviour. He described 27 fundamental activities controlling everything from friendship to murder. He contended that variations in the external surface of the skull were caused by pressure exerted internally by brain activity.

Gall's research and intensity of purpose were directed to the brain as the organ determining individual human characteristics. Some believed this was the beginning of neuropsychology as a science, while others were more sceptical. At any rate, Gall's ideas fell into disrepute, although he might be regarded as a researcher whose work focussed attention on the newly emerging disciplines seeking to understand human activities and thought processes.

GALTON, Sir Francis (1822-1911)

A "gentleman scientist", trained in medicine who developed an interest in anthropology and criminology. He came from a wealthy background and had the resources to travel widely to secure ideas and information. He was also a very able statistician.

Galton was initially drawn to **Bertillon**'s system of anthropometry which was sweeping across Europe in the late nineteenth century. He set up an anthropometry laboratory in London in 1884 and became acquainted with fingerprints through William **Herschel**. With his mathematical turn of mind, Galton could see the potential that fingerprinting had to offer as a quicker and easier means of identification than Bertillon's system.

In 1888, the British government, undecided about which of the competing systems to adopt, asked Galton to go to Paris, talk to Bertillon and report his findings. He returned to London convinced that fingerprint identification was the right way and reported as such to the Royal Institution.

Galton believed there were too many variables in the measurement system which Bertillon had devised, whereas fingerprints offered greater precision. He set out to prove this statistically and determined that, using an individual's ten fingerprints, meant that the chances of two persons having the same prints were 64,000,000,000 to 1. He published his work in 1892 in a book simply called, *Finger Prints*. This excited attention around the world and not least in Argentina where Juan **Vucetich** was poised to make history using fingerprints recovered from a crime scene which were used to identify a murderer.

Galton worked with Sir Edward **Henry** to devise a system of classification which was eventually adopted by Scotland Yard and by police forces worldwide. He won many accolades for his work including admission to the Royal Society in 1856.

While his contribution to criminology was immense, Galton is also remembered for his work on eugenics, part of his studies in measuring the inborn differences between human individuals. His life's work was really his fascination with measurement which he applied to many disciplines. It was perhaps fitting that Karl **Pearson**, a fellow statistician, should write about Galton's life in a three volume study published in 1930.

GERASIMOV, Mikhail (1907-1970)

Russian palaeontologist who pioneered facial reconstruction. By examining the correlation between the skull and the face, he showed it was possible to build a living likeness from skeletal remains.

Gerasimov studied medicine at Irkutsk in Russia and became involved in a project to reconstruct the faces of prehistorical human beings. His first successes came in 1927 with reconstructions of Neanderthal man and Pithecanthropus. He developed a system of gauging the thickness of the soft tissues on the face from the underlying skull and, by employing plastic modelling techniques, re-created life-like features.

Gerasimov's work, popularly described as face-from-the-skull reconstruction, was successfully used in an historical context but, increasingly, he was called on to apply his skills to crime investigation. His life-like recreations of the appearance of unidentified and long dead individuals provided answers to previously unsolved crimes.

He gained international recognition for his work and, in 1950, founded the Laboratory for Plastic Reconstruction at the USSR Academy of Sciences. His book, *Basic Principles of Facial Reconstruction from the Cranium*, was published around the same time, confirming Russia's lead in this field.

GETTLER, Dr. Alexander (1883-1968)

Toxicologist and chemist who worked in the New York medical examiner's office for forty-one years. He also taught chemistry at New York University.

Dr. Gettler is credited with devising a method for determining death by drowning. He showed that a higher concentration of chloride electrolytes entering the lungs from drowning in sea water would be found in the blood on the left side of the heart, and, conversely, in the right side if drowning occurred in fresh water. He published his study of this phenomenon in *A Method for Determination of Death by Drowning* in 1921.

In 1942, he was consulted about the discovery of a woman's body in New York's Central Park. The chief suspect was her husband, Terry Almodovar, who denied having been at the crime scene. Dr. Gettler took soil samples at the scene and found some unusual grass seeds. The same variety of seeds were found on Almodovar's clothing.

A botanist identified the seeds as a rare species known to grow in only one place in the whole of New York – Central Park. Detectives were told that this particular grass seed flowered later than most and could not have been transferred before mid-October. The murdered woman's body was found in early November. Botanical evidence thereby linked the suspect to the crime scene.

GLAISTER, Professor John (1892-1971)

After qualification in 1916, John Glaister served as an army medic and, at the conclusion of World War One, went into general practice. He pursued this for a short while and then decided he wanted to follow a career in forensic medicine.

He had developed an interest in trace evidence and, in particular, the possibilities offered by hair analysis in the investigation of crime. He made a detailed study of the differences between hairs of human and animal origin. Over several years, he compiled a collection of over a thousand microphotographs of hair samples and published them in book form in 1931. This study was destined to become a standard reference work and, in the year of publication, he was appointed professor of forensic medicine at Glasgow University as successor to his father.

In 1935, Professor Glaister was involved in a sensational murder case when a fellow medic, Dr. Buck Ruxton, who practised in Lancaster, was charged with killing his wife and her maid. When the dismembered remains of two women were found in a Scottish river, the task of identifying them fell to Glaister.

Aided by an anatomist, Professor James Couper **Brash**, Glaister set about the task of re-assembling the body parts, chiefly the skeletal remains. Their painstaking work was capped by a pioneering innovation. By superimposing studio portrait photographs of the two women on X-ray photographs of the skulls, they were able to confirm their identities.

Glaister and his university colleagues also made use of the emerging potential of forensic entomology by examining maggots retrieved from the corpses. Using knowledge of the life cycle, they were able to calculate the length of time since the victims had died. The forensic story complete, Glaister gave evidence at Ruxton's trial which resulted in a guilty verdict.

He subsequently gave expert testimony in a number of murder trials, as well as keeping himself occupied with his pen. In 1937, *The Medico-Legal Aspects of the Ruxton Case* by Glaister and Brash was published. Other books followed, including *The Power of Poison* (1954) and *Final Diagnosis* (1964) as well as the editorship of his father's work *Glaister's Medical Jurisprudence and Toxicology* which went to numerous editions.

John Glaister's achievement in a lifetime devoted to forensic work was to show the potential of combining science, medicine and the law. He was a strong advocate of setting up a unified medico-legal institution in the UK. No doubt to his satisfaction, this was established during his retirement years.

GODDARD, Dr. Calvin H. (1891-1955)

After qualifying as a doctor, Goddard was commissioned in the US army at the outbreak of World War One. He worked in ordnance and developed a life-long interest in firearms. He became the foremost authority on forensic ballistics in the USA and was editor of the *American Journal of Police Science*.

Goddard was the first internationally recognised authority on firearms identification and perfected **Gravelle**'s comparison microscope, turning it into a sensitive tool that revolutionised forensic ballistics. The technology was described in *The Journal of Criminal Law Criminology* in 1926.

In 1920, two Italian immigrants carried out a payroll raid in South Braintree, Massachusetts, which ended in double murder. Nicola Sacco and Bartolomeo Vanzetti were quickly rounded up and charged with murder. The trial of the two men made a big impact at the time, not least because of the hostility directed at them by the public.

The trial took place before the advent of the comparison

microscope and the new science of forensic ballistics was very much itself on trial. The experts at the time were inexperienced but their testimony was sufficient to persuade the jury to bring in a guilty verdict. Sacco and Vanzetti were sentenced to death.

The outcome of the trial was widely reported and unease grew about executing the two men on the basis of disputed evidence. After many delays and much hesitation, Dr. Goddard was called on by the prosecutor's office for his opinion.

Using his comparison microscope to examine the crime scene bullets, he determined that one of them had been fired by Sacco's pistol and could not have been discharged from any other weapon. One of the defence experts viewing Goddard's demonstration, agreed with the correction of his assessment. In consequence, death sentences on Sacco and Vanzetti were carried out in August 1927.

Goddard's reputation was such that he was appointed Director of a new Scientific Crime Detection Laboratory in Illinois. America's pre-eminence in the field of forensic ballistics was assured and the FBI set up its own department for testing firearms evidence in 1931. Five years later, Goddard published his seminal work, *The History of Firearms Identification*.

GOFF, Dr. M. Lee

Professor of Entomology at the University of Hawaii who played a leading role in persuading police and crime agencies in the USA to adopt forensic entomology as part of investigative procedure.

That post mortem interval could be determined by studying the succession patterns of insects on dead bodies was noted in 1855 by Dr. Louis **Bergeret** in France. In a body reduced to skeletal remains, insect evidence may provide the only reliable estimate of the time elapsed since death occurred.

Dr. Goff takes the view that while "most maggots look a lot alike", they have a story to tell. Evidence of insect activity during the early phases of decomposition may indicate the presence of ante mortem or peri mortem wounds that are no longer visible.

Furthermore, maggots feeding off a dead body absorb any toxins that may be present in the decomposing remains and, on toxicological analysis, may indicate that drugs or toxins have contributed to death. In this respect, maggots feeding on a corpse effectively become part of that body's tissues.

In 2000, Dr. Goff published *A Fly For The Prosecution* in which he explained how insect evidence helps to solve crimes.

GONZALES, Dr. Thomas A. (1878-1956)

A leading US forensic pathologist who worked as assistant to Dr. Charles **Norris** whom he succeeded as Chief Medical Examiner for New York City in 1937. Like his predecessor, Gonzales was prepared to challenge first assumptions in order to reach the truth. He was particularly adept at distinguishing between accident, suicide and murder as his case files testified. He was especially knowledgeable about knife wounds.

With fellow pathologists, Morgan Vance and Milton **Helpern**, he wrote *Legal Medicine and Toxicology*, a book first published in 1937. Amounting to over a thousand printed pages, and providing a practical guide for working pathologists, this was an immense undertaking. The guide was widely praised and not least for confirming New York's credentials as a leading centre for forensic excellence.

Following in the footsteps of his mentor, Gonzales succeeded Dr. Norris as Professor at New York University's Medical School, retiring in 1954.

GRADWOHL, Dr. Rutherford B.H. (1877-1959)

Trained as a clinical pathologist, he spent time in Europe and gravitated towards forensic medicine. During the First World War, he served with the US Navy Medical Corps. In due course, he was appointed Professor of Bacteriology and Pathology at what became St Louis University School of Medicine.

Gradwohl's studies abroad drew him in to the world of forensics and he became such an asset to the St Louis Police Department that in 1934 he was asked to set up a police crime laboratory. The work of the laboratory was held in high esteem, not just in the USA, but also internationally.

In 1948, he was a key figure in establishing the American Academy of Forensic Sciences which was considered a model of its kind. Dr.

Gradwohl's achievements were admired internationally and among his many visitors was Professor Francis **Camps**, the UK pathologist who would establish a parallel institution in Britain.

Dr. Gradwohl published an influential textbook in 1954 entitled, *Legal Medicine*, which was justifiably regarded as an encyclopaedia. And, in the spirit of cooperation between the USA and Europe, he invited Camps to succeed him as editor.

Gradwohl retired in 1959 and died in the same year.

GRANT, Dr. Julius (1902-1991)

A chemist who worked for over fifty years in the paper-making business. He came to prominence in his role as a private consultant when he debunked the authenticity of the diaries attributed to Mussolini in 1967 and Hitler in 1983.

In the case of Mussolini's alleged diaries, Dr. Grant showed that the paper written on to produce the volume for 1925 had not been used in Italy before 1937. When asked to examine the Hitler diaries, he proved that the paper they were written on had been manufactured after Hitler's death in 1945.

Dr. Grant served as President of both the Forensic Science Society and the Medico-Legal Society.

GRAVELLE, Philip O.

Pioneering inventor in the USA of the comparison microscope which turned forensic ballistics into a science. He was influenced by Charles **Waite**'s contention that firearms had individual characteristics which left identifiable marks on bullets fired from them.

Working with John H. Fisher, Gravelle developed the helixometer, a device which made it possible to look inside a gun barrel and examine its spiral grooving. The helixometer owed its origins to the cystoscopy instruments used in hospitals to inspect internal body organs.

The next step was the construction of a measuring microscope that would allow the lands and grooves in a weapon's rifling to be measured and recorded. Allied to this was Gravelle's skill with a camera which he used to photograph bullets test-fired from various weapons. By comparing the marks made on the bullets, he was able to match their distinctive characteristics to a particular firearm.

The next step was to find a way of creating a ballistic fingerprint which was achieved with the development of the comparison microscope. This allowed two images to be viewed side-by-side for direct comparison. Thus it became possible to view a crime bullet and a bullet test-fired from a suspected murder weapon together in the same field of vision.

This was ground-breaking science achieved by team work which others, including Calvin **Goddard**, would build on to perfect comparative microscopy. Forensic ballistics thus became a powerful tool aiding crime investigation.

GROSS, Dr. Hans (1847-1915)

Austrian magistrate who played a pivotal role in establishing science-based crime investigation methods in police work. The time he spent in the law courts made him realise that a successful criminal justice system needed a more reliable foundation than evidence provided by informers and confessions.

Although not trained in any scientific discipline, Gross was blessed with consummate powers of observation and deduction. His thinking was said to have been prompted by an injury sustained by his grandfather while serving in the Austrian army. The soldier was shot in the eye with a musket ball which did not kill him but left surgeons with a dilemma. Should they attempt to remove the projectile or leave it? They decided against removal and it remained in the eye socket until the man died in old age.

After his death, the musket ball was retrieved and Gross examined it closely. He noticed that it was scored with marks made by the weapon which fired it and it even carried traces of powder embedded in its surface. Gross was astute enough to realise that such traces could be put to good use as evidence. Thus began his life-long interest in forensic ballistics.

Dr. Gross schooled himself in the major scientific disciplines to which he added photography and microscopy for good measure. Over a period of twenty years, while serving as a magistrate, he compiled information for what would become virtually the Bible of criminalistics. In 1893, he published his landmark book, *System der Kriminalistik* which, for the first time, set out scientific procedures for investigating crime.

GUSTAFSON, Dr. Gösta (1906-2001)

Internationally recognised forensic odontologist who served as Professor of Oral Pathology at Lund University for over twenty years. He published a landmark textbook in 1966 entitled, *Forensic Odontology*, which was the first time the subject had been set out comprehensively in the English Language.

Gustafson was particularly adept at estimating age from the teeth and the appearance of marks in the mouth indicative of particular occupations and trades. Craftsmen who habitually used nails and screws frequently held them in their mouth while working, thereby creating distinctive patterns of wear. Similarly, musicians performing with wind instruments incurred characteristic marks in their mouths.

Teeth have long been used as a means of identifying dead bodies and Gustafson said that the science of odontology was such that particular schools of dentistry or even, individual dentists, could be identified by their work on an individual's teeth. This was born out in the Christie case in 1953 when a crowned tooth in the jaw of one of the sets of human remains found at 10 Rillington Place was identified as the work of an Austrian dental practice. The victim proved to be an Austrian refugee.

Forensic dentistry was well established in Scandinavia and Professor Gustafson was one of its pioneers. He established the Scandinavian Society of Forensic Dentistry in 1961 and was the co-founder of the international organisation set up to advance ondontological evidence.

HEINDL, Dr. Robert (1883-1958)

Pioneering criminologist who played a major role in introducing fingerprint examination in Germany. Inspired by Sir Edward **Henry**'s work on dactyloscopy, Heindl carried out his own research on methods of taking and storing fingerprints.

He set up a police laboratory in Dresden in 1915 and, at the end of World War One, moved to Berlin as a centre for his influence in persuading police forces in Germany to adopt the fingerprint classification system which had been perfected in England.

In 1927, he published a guide to fingerprint identification entitled, *System und Praxis der Daktyloscopie* and worked on the late Dr. Hans **Gross**'s criminological archives. Dr. Heindl came out of retirement in 1946 and returned to work in Munich where he set up a crime laboratory and worked as head of the Bavarian Central Police Institute.

In a career spanning two world wars, he established a practical approach to recording fingerprints for subsequent examination and comparison in criminal investigations.

HEINRICH, Dr. Edward Oscar (1881-1953)

Pioneering US criminologist working initially as a private consultant while lecturing at Berkeley, California. He was endowed with many skills, principally in the fields of chemistry and biology. He was an acknowledged authority on questioned documents.

During his professional career, Dr. Heinrich contributed to many crime investigations but one in particular stands out. In 1923, a mail train was hijacked by three armed robbers in the mountains of southern Oregon. They blew up the mail car, shot dead the driver, fireman and brakeman before fleeing the scene. The robbers left behind weapons and discarded a pair of overalls which would prove to be of major significance.

Heinrich was called in to assist the police investigation and his attention was immediately drawn to the overalls. He read them like a book, unveiling details about the individual who had worn them. Heinrich told investigators to look for a left-handed lumberjack who worked with fir trees, was slight in stature with light-coloured hair and rolled his own cigarettes. He said the man was in his early twenties and stood about 5 feet 10 inches in height.

Detectives were astonished by this precise description which the astute criminologist had provided. Heinrich had readily identified Douglas fir needles in the pockets of the overalls and noted that the garment was regularly buttoned in a fashion which suggested left-handedness. A piece of paper which had survived several launderings was found in one of the pockets. Faded writing on it was enhanced by treatment with iodine vapour and identified as a receipt which was traced to Roy d'Autrement who, with his two brothers, proved to be the train robbers. They faced justice for their crime and Heinrich found fame.

He had pulled off an amazing piece of criminological detection based on his belief that every criminal leaves behind evidence of his presence at the crime scene. Heinrich became Professor of Criminology at the University of California and continued to advise US police departments on the scientific aspects of their investigations.

HELPERN, Dr. Milton (1902-1977)

In his half century of work as a pathologist, Dr. Helpern served as Chief Medical Examiner for New York City for twenty years. He was highly respected for his work and not least for his prodigious output of articles for the medical press. In 1962, the Milton Helpern Legal Medical Library, the first collection of its kind in the USA, was inaugurated.

Dr. Helpern worked on some notorious and controversial cases, and none more so that that of Dr. Carl Coppolino, an anaesthetist charged with murder in 1965. When his wife died, supposedly of a heart attack, Coppolino remarried within three weeks. There were reports that he had been treating her with succinylcholine chloride, a muscle relaxant used in surgery, which killed her. Suspicions were aroused when the widow of a former patient accused him of murder.

This led to the exhumation of the body and Dr. Helpern was called in to carry out the post mortem. He found evidence of needle marks on the corpse and took tissue samples. These were analysed using state-of-the-art toxicological methods to determine whether the dead woman had been injected with succinylcholine. The difficulty was that, once administered, the drug breaks down rapidly in the body. Nevertheless, toxicologists found abnormal amounts of succinic acid in the body which led to Coppolino being put on trial in 1967 for murdering his wife.

The evidence was mostly circumstantial and led to acrimonious exchanges in court. The defence contended that no reliable evidence regarding cause of death had been established by the forensic specialists. The jury went with the science and found the defendant guilty of murder.

Writing later in his book of memoirs, entitled *Autopsy*, published in 1977, Dr. Helpern commented on the art of being an expert witness and searching for the truth. He quoted the French medico-legal pioneer, Paul **Brouardel**, who wrote, "If the law has made you a witness, remain a man of science". Milton Helpern certainly lived up to that.

Much earlier in his career, along with three other doctors, Helpern compiled *Legal Medicine and Toxicology*, published in 1937, which became a standard textbook for training young pathologists. His legacy was that his work helped to consolidate the learning needed to practise as a forensic pathologist.

HENRY, Sir Edward
(1850-1931)

Following studies made by **Faulds**, **Galton** and **Herschel**, Henry put into place the final piece of the jigsaw that made identification of fingerprints a working system. While serving as Inspector General of Police in Nepal in the 1890's, he used Bertillon's system as a means of identifying criminals. His feeling was that the process was too complicated and prone to error. When he read Galton's book on fingerprints, he instinctively felt it was a better system.

Henry liaised with Galton and the two men shared ideas. Henry determined that there were five distinct patterns present in every set of fingerprints and he resolved to find a way of classifying them. Legend has it that his moment of inspiration came during a rail journey in India in 1896. Lacking paper to write on, he scribbled a few notes on his shirt cuff. Like Galton, he had noted that the tip of each finger contained triangular segments, which he called deltas at the point where ridge patterns met the transverse capillary lines. Henry's insight was that this unique configuration could be measured and classified by means of a simple mathematical formula.

In 1898, he published his book, *The Classification and Uses of Finger Prints*, by which time the Government of India had rejected Bertillon's anthropometric system and replaced it with Galton and Henry's dactyloscopy. In 1900, the British Government followed suit and Henry was appointed Assistant Commissioner at Scotland Yard in charge of the Central Fingerprint Bureau. In 1902, came the first criminal conviction using fingerprints retrieved from the scene of a burglary and, in 1905, the first conviction using fingerprint evidence in a murder case.

News of Henry's classification quickly spread to police forces around the world and, in 1906, Lieutenant Joseph **Faurot** of the New York Police Department visited England to gain first-hand experience. By 1914, fingerprint identification prevailed worldwide.

Sir Edward Henry's book on fingerprint classification remained a standard text for many years. In 1903, he was appointed Commissioner of London's Metropolitan Police and served with distinction until he retired in 1918.

HERSCHEL, Sir William (1833-1917)

In the 1850s, Herschel was posted to India as a colonial administrator. He made a practice of insisting that his Indian workers "signed" contracts by pressing their inked palms onto written agreements. He soon discovered that single fingerprints were as distinctive as whole handprints.

When appointed a magistrate in 1877, he used fingerprints to verify the identity of prison inmates. That year, he wrote to the Inspector General of Prisons seeking the wider recognition of fingerprinting. He said that, after twenty years' experience using what he called "sign manuals", he could vouch for the identity of every individual whose fingerprints had been recorded.

Herschel's suggestion was turned down but his letter clearly established him as the first person to recognise the identification potential of fingerprints. Continuing his studies, he went on to establish that an individual's skin impressions remained constant throughout life.

Having being rebuffed by officialdom and in poor health, Herschel returned to England in 1879 and soon became embroiled in the controversy initiated by Henry **Faulds**. At the root of this was the fact that, while Herschel had undoubtedly seen the significance of fingerprint identification many years before Faulds, he had not published the results of his studies.

Herschel went on to collaborate with Francis **Galton**, sharing knowledge and establishing his rightful place as one of the pioneers of fingerprinting.

HOLZER, Dr. Franz Josef (1903-1974)

Leading Austrian forensic scientist who played an important role in the development of serology. Working at the Institute of Forensic Medicine in Innsbruck in the early 1930's, he carried out research on the problems involved in detecting the blood group characteristics of stains of unknown origin.

Building on the work of **Leone Lattes** and others, he concentrated on finding agglutinins using a multiple dilution technique. Holzer's absorption test was used successfully in a murder case in 1931. A farmer in a rural community had been robbed and killed in an attack with an axe. The chief suspect was the man's step brother who denied killing but was unable to explain the bloodstains on his clothing.

Holzer applied his test method to the stains and determined that they were blood group O, the same as the murder victim, whereas the suspect was group A. Confronted with this evidence, the brother-in-law made a confession. Following this success, Holzer's absorption method was widely adopted for use in forensic investigation of suspicious stains.

In 1933, he travelled to the USA to work in New York with the legendary Karl **Landsteiner** to further advance his blood grouping techniques. Holzer later moved to Berlin where he set up a research laboratory at the University's Institute for Forensic and Social Medicine. Prior to the outbreak of World War Two, he worked on defining sub-groups and other factors which determined blood grouping characteristics.

HRDLICKA, Ales (1869-1943)

Czech-born scientist who put the subject of physical anthropology firmly on the map in America and established himself as a leading authority. He emigrated to the USA in the 1880s where he studied medicine at Baltimore.

Uncertain as to the course he wanted to follow in his professional life, he took a job in a mental institution where he learned the essentials of Bertillon's method of anthropometry. In the late 1890s, he worked as an anthropologist in Paris.

When he returned to the USA, Hrdlicka started his own laboratory and began collecting anthropological data about native Americans. He also travelled extensively, collecting information and artefacts to broaden his understanding. In 1903 he was appointed the first curator of physical anthropology at the Smithsonian Institution in Washington DC.

During the next forty years, he built up the most comprehensive collection of anthropological material in the world at that time. A significant part of the collection was human skeletal material used as teaching media. His services were called upon by the FBI to help solve criminal cases involving human skeletal remains. He also founded and edited the *American Journal of Physical Anthropology*.

Hrdlicka was a highly influential figure in the American science scene and his work forged a path for forensic anthropology which assumed considerable importance during the next century. His work was the springboard for a generation of American anthropologists who would come to be called "bone doctors".

JEFFREYS, Professor Sir Alec (1950-)

Professor of Genetics at the University of Leicester, Alec Jeffreys gained worldwide recognition with his development in 1984 of DNA fingerprinting.

His genetic studies led him to the realisation that variations in the human genetic code could be used to identify individuals. He recognised the immense potential of his research which was quickly used to good effect to trap a double murderer.

The murders of two teenage girls, three years apart, in the Narborough area taxed the resources of the Leicestershire police who feared the killer might strike again. Both victims had been raped and strangled and semen traces left on their bodies. Following Jeffreys' discovery that every individual could be identified by means of the unique genetic material in body tissues, blood, saliva and semen, it was decided to employ DNA fingerprints in the search for the murderer.

A mass blood sampling exercise involving 4,000 males aged between seventeen and thirty-four was organised but failed to produce a positive result. Then, by chance, it was learnt that a man who should have given a blood sample, had arranged for someone else to take his place. That person was Colin Pitchfork whose blood when it was eventually sampled was found to match the DNA characteristics of the murderer.

This was a double triumph for DNA testing because, in addition to identifying the killer, it also exonerated an innocent suspect who had falsely confessed to the crimes. Pitchfork was tried for double murder in 1988 and found guilty.

Professor Jeffreys' discovery revolutionised the process of identifying human individuals and not just in criminal cases. DNA fingerprinting became an important tool used to identify people who had died in circumstances which rendered them unrecognisable, as a result of both natural and man-made disasters, such as fires and aviation accidents.

Sir Alec gained many plaudits for his discovery and also international honours. He continues his research work on human genetics.

JESERICH, Dr. Paul (1854-1927)

One of the pioneers of forensic chemistry working at the University of Berlin in the 1880s who used photographic methods to examine a range of crime scene evidence. Jeserich began his professional career in the food industry but decided to devote his attention to the forensic uses of chemistry.

He showed considerable versatility, studying bloodstains, testing for poisons, examining documents, textiles, hair and firearms. As his reputation grew, he came to be known as the "German Sherlock Holmes".

In 1904, he became involved in a high profile murder case when the body of a young girl was found in the River Spree in Berlin. She had been reported missing from home and, evidently, had been raped. Suspicion fell on a man called Theodor Berger who lived with a prostitute in the same apartment building as the dead girl.

Detectives searched Berger's rooms and found some bloodstained clothing. Dr. Jeserich examined the garments using the blood sampling methods developed by Paul **Uhlenhuth**. By these means, he determined that the stains were not of human origin. A breakthrough in the investigation came when police found a suitcase containing clothing bearing bloodstains and fibres which matched the dead girl's skirt.

Berger protested his innocence but the scientific evidence told against him. Jeserich acknowledged the influence of Dr. Hans **Gross** and, particularly, the emphasis he placed on textile and fibre trace evidence. In a long career, Jeserich mastered all the arts of forensic chemistry, especially the value of microphotography as a tool for comparing and recording evidence.

KEELER, Dr. Leonarde (1903-1949)

Foremost authority on testing for deception, he developed the lie detector in 1921 in association with Dr. John A. Larson. The concept of detecting lies when criminal suspects were being questioned had been pursued in Europe and the USA since the early 1900s.

Encouraged by August **Vollmer**, Police Chief at Berkeley, California, Keeler and Larson conceived the first lie detector in 1921. This was a machine which recorded variations in a person's blood pressure and respiration while being questioned. Pen recorders traced the responses on paper scrolls which were then scrutinised by trained operators.

With further developments, a more sophisticated machine called a polygraph emerged to mixed fortunes. The device proved fallible to the extent that seasoned criminals proved guilty by other means found ways of outwitting the device.

Advocates of the polygraph urged for the acceptance of lie

detection findings to be admissible as evidence in court cases. To the disappointment of Keeler and others, this did not happen, at least, not without firm strictures. Polygraph evidence only became admissible in US courts when both prosecution and defence agreed on its use or when the judge requested it. Nevertheless, polygraph systems are used routinely by businesses and government agencies to screen job applications.

KERSTA, Lawrence G (1907-1994)

Researcher at Bell Telephone who originated the concept of the voiceprint as a means of identification in the 1960s. His studies led him to the view that each human voice was unique in terms of resonance, pitch and volume.

Kersta developed a recording technique which produced a sound spectrograph uniquely characteristic of the speaker. Voices recorded in this way made a visible record which could be reliably identified. The hope was that voiceprinting would be accepted as an indicator of identity in much the same way as a fingerprint.

The admissibility of voiceprints as evidence in court proved to be controversial. Difficulties lay more with interpreting the results than with the principles involved. In due course, police forces in the USA took up voiceprint identification, particularly in crime cases involving telephone and voice messages.

KIRK, Dr. Paul Leland (1902-1970)

Professor of Criminalistics at the University of California, Berkeley, for forty-three years. In association with August **Vollmer**, Berkeley's pioneering police official, he set up his school of criminology in 1950. It rapidly became a centre of excellence and Kirk's book, *Crime Investigation*, published in 1953, was a leading textbook for many years.

Dr. Kirk trained as a biochemist and his early work experience was on the Manhattan Project, led by Professor Oppenheimer. At the conclusion of World War Two, he turned to criminology and became a pioneer of blood spatter analysis raising its importance as evidence in crime scene investigation.

He came to prominence in 1954 at the time of the Sheppard

murder case in Cleveland. Marylin Sheppard had been found battered to death in her bedroom. She had been savagely beaten and her head smashed with a blunt instrument. Suspicion fell on her husband, Dr. Sam Sheppard, who was convicted of second-degree murder on the basis of dubious evidence.

Many months afterwards, Dr. Kirk was called on to make a re-assessment of the crime scene. By examining the blood spatters, he was able to determine the sequence of events on the night in question. There were no traces of blood on the ceiling of the room, whereas blood had been deposited on the walls. From this, he concluded that the murder weapon had been wielded in a horizontal fashion, swinging backwards and forwards to strike the victim's head.

Kirk judged that the killer had stood between the twin beds in the murder room and noted blood on the right side of the victim's head. The killer's body had shielded the walls behind him thereby preventing flying blood spatters on these surfaces. The criminologist further concluded that, standing in the position indicated by the blood patterns, the killer, probably left-handed, would have been heavily bloodstained. When interviewed by the police, Dr. Sheppard was found to have a bloodstain on his trousers and, more significantly, was shown not to be left-handed.

Twelve years after his wife's violent death, Dr. Sheppard was granted a second trial which aired the new evidence, and he was found not guilty. Dr. Kirk's analysis of the blood spatter patterns at the crime scene proved crucial in securing Sheppard's innocence. One of the implications of the re-trial was to show that previous attitudes to crime scene investigation were out-moded and that law officers and forensic experts with appropriate training should be employed in major investigations.

KOCKEL, Dr. Richard (1865-1934)

Leading forensic pathologist in Germany in the early part of the twentieth century. He represented a new generation of medical examiner who stressed the importance of doctors called to attend crime scenes having training in forensic procedures.

Kockel's ideas did not meet with approval from the medical

establishment but he proved his point in a 1929 murder case while working in the Institute of Forensic Medicine at Leipzig University. He was called out to what the police believed was a road accident in which the driver of a car was burned to death when the vehicle caught fire.

The driver was believed to be a local businessman who had met a tragic death and the body was released for burial. Suspicion was aroused, though, when it was learned that his widow had cashed in on a recently taken out insurance policy. The body was exhumed and Dr. Kockel carried out a post mortem examination. He found no evidence of sooty deposits in the air passages and no traces of carbon monoxide in the blood. The pathologist found fatty embolisms in the blood vessels which were indicative of violent trauma. His conclusion was that the dead man had been murdered before being incinerated.

His conclusions were borne out when the missing businessman turned up alive and well and, following police questioning, admitted to killing a hitchhiker and staging the fire in order to claim on the insurance. Erich Tetzner was subsequently convicted of murder, thanks mainly to the shrewd investigative work of Dr. Kockel. The pathologist had dramatically reinforced his point about the need for crime scene doctors to have forensic training.

KOEHLER, Arthur (1885-1967)

Foremost US expert on timber products, using knowledge of cellular structure, growth rings and, particularly, machining and tool marks. He worked for thirty-six years in the US Forestry Service and was the author of *The Uses and Properties of Wood*. He gave evidence in a number of criminal cases which earned him the title, "wood detective".

Koehler came to prominence in 1932 when he played a key role in the Lindbergh kidnapping case. When Charles Lindbergh's son was taken from his home, footprints were found near the house, together with a broken ladder which had been used to access the child's bedroom. There was also a ransom note.

The "wood detective" spent more than a year tracing the source of the timber used to construct the homemade ladder. He found distinctive marks on the wood made by a planing machine. On close examination he was able to identify the type of plane used and observed that it had a damaged blade which left identifiable marks. By dogged persistence, he found a timber mill in South Carolina which had machined the wood used to make the ladder.

By this time the police had taken prime suspect, Bruno Hauptmann, into custody and Koehler made a visit to his home. He found nail holes punched in the floor which exactly matched the nails on the ladder and also found that a piece of wooden flooring had been used to finalise its construction. In Hauptmann's workshop, he discovered a wood plane that had made identifiable marks on the rungs of the ladder.

In due course, Hauptmann was brought to trial and convicted of murder. His attorney scoffed at the idea of a "wood expert" giving testimony, declaring it was not a science like fingerprinting or ballistics. Koehler proved how wrong he was in making this assertion.

KROGMAN, Dr. Wilton Marion (1903-1987)

One of the pioneers of physical anthropology in the USA and author of the influential *Guide to the Identification of Human Skeletal Material*, published by the FBI in 1939. His work provided the foundation for methods of identifying otherwise unknown war dead from the battlefields of Europe and, later, Korea.

In the 1930s, Dr. Krogman's expertise was used by the FBI to resolve identification problems resulting from crime investigation. His work gave rise to the emergence of the science of forensic anthropology. He followed a successful teaching career in Chicago and was appointed Professor of Physical Anthropology at the University of Pennsylvania in 1947. Among his published works are *The Growth of Man* (1941) and *The Human Skeleton in Forensic Medicine* (1986).

His work won increasing recognition in the aftermath of various conflicts involving the recovered remains of unidentified service personnel. His work provided closure for many grieving families. One of the forensic puzzles he helped to solve was the identification of the long-buried bodies of the Russian Czar, Nicholas II and his family.

LACASSAGNE, Alexandre (1843-1924)

One of the great practitioners of forensic medicine who pioneered new methods and new ways of thinking. He served with the French navy in North Africa where he developed an interest in those characteristics of sudden death that would help doctors in their investigations.

He made a special study of tattoos, realising their relevance to establishing identity. He also studied rigor mortis, body cooling, and lividity as means of determining time of death. When he turned his mind to firearms, he observed that marks left on a bullet might be related to the weapon from which it was discharged.

Lacassagne was appointed Professor of Pathology and Forensic Medicine at the University of Lyon in 1880 where one of his pupils was Edmond **Locard** who was destined to make a special contribution to the world of forensic studies. Lacassagne published his seminal work, *Précis de Médecine Judiciare* in 1878 and was poised to become involved in a case that established his public recognition.

When the decaying remains of a man's body were found near Lyon, inquiries suggested he might be a court bailiff by the name of Gouffé who had been missing for over a year. A relative was unable to identify the remains which left the police investigation to Lacassagne. He had already determined that the dead man had been strangled and set about establishing details that might lead to identification.

By measuring the long bones, he estimated height at about five feet eight inches which closely matched that of Gouffé. By examining the teeth, he estimated age at about fifty years which, again matched the missing bailiff's age. Significantly, he observed a deformity in the leg bones which would have resulted in a limp.

This too was a matching feature. In a final flourish, Lacassagne compared the hair of the corpse with hair taken from a brush found in Gouffé's apartment – it matched. Beyond doubt, the identity of the dead man had been established.

Using this information, the police stepped up their enquiries and rounded up two individuals who confessed to murdering Gouffé and disposing of his body.

Lacassagne's forensic work had been a triumph and his combination of bone studies, dental and hair comparisons and other features brought him personal fame. On a broader canvas, it put criminology and forensic investigation into the public domain. His philosophy, echoed by many who followed him was, "One must know how to doubt".

LANDSTEINER, Dr. Karl (1868-1943)

One of the great medical pioneers working in the field of immunology and serology. His discovery of blood groups facilitated many medical advances, including safe procedures for blood transfusion. The ability to identify an individual's blood group also provided crime investigators with a powerful tool with which to eliminate or incriminate suspects.

Landsteiner worked at the Institute of Pathology and Anatomy at Vienna University when, in 1901, he discovered that the blood of every human individual could be categorised under four types depending on the presence or absence of two antigens in the red corpuscles. He called these Groups, A, B, AB and O.

The importance of this discovery was overlooked at the time and it fell to the Italian serologist, Leone **Lattes**, several years later, to build on Landsteiner's achievement. Further blood groups were discovered, including factors M and N and, in 1937, the Rhesus Factor.

Landsteiner carried on his development work in the USA at the Rockefeller Institute of Medical Research in New York. He was acknowledged as a teacher and respected for his willingness to share his knowledge. He published his early work in 1900 and subsequently shared his authorship with co-workers. In 1930, he was nominated for the Nobel Prize for Physiology and Medicine.

LATTES, Leone (1887-1954)

Leading forensic serologist who developed a method for identifying blood groups in old, dried stains. He studied at Turin under Cesare **Lombroso** and gained distinction as a professor of forensic medicine.

In 1915, he showed that it was possible to determine blood grouping in three-month old stains based on the presence of agglutinins in blood serum. He continually refined his methods and, in 1922, published a book, *The Individuality of Blood*, and, in the following year, successfully tested twelve-month old bloodstains in a criminal investigation which led to a murder conviction.

Lattes's methods were widely adopted and, in 1925, the German Society of Forensic Medicine honoured him for his pioneering work. He acknowledged the lead given in this field by Dr. Paul **Uhlenhuth** and continued to develop and extend his methods, achieving success in the examination of ever older bloodstains and small amounts of residue.

His work led to the important discovery that other body fluids, such as semen, sweat and saliva, could also be tested for blood group characteristics. This was a significant advance in the scientific investigation of crime.

LEE, Dr. Henry C (1938-)

One of America's foremost crime scientists known to his contemporaries as, "king of the crime scene". Born in China, he moved to the USA in 1945 and studied forensic science and biochemistry at New York University. He went on to revolutionise approaches to crime scene investigation, improving existing methods and adopting new technology which combined the best forensic disciplines available.

In 1979, Dr. Lee was appointed Director of the Connecticut State Police Forensic Science Laboratory when he established himself as a teacher and specialist consultant. He featured in a number of high profile cases including the disappearance in 1986 of a Pan Am air stewardess. Suspicion centred on her husband, Richard Crafts.

A witness came forward to report that he had seen Crafts operating a wood chipper at a riverside location close to his home.

It was established that Crafts had recently bought the wood chipper together with rubber gloves and a spade. Dr. Lee examined the riverside site and found bone fragments, part of a tooth and the remains of a finger. The tooth fragment was sufficient to identify the victim and, after due process, Crafts was found guilty of murder.

Dr. Lee's high profile cases included the trial of O.J. Simpson in 1994 at a time when he was established as a leading crime consultant. He published *Henry Lee's Crime Scene Handbook* in 2001 and *Blood Evidence and DNA* in 2003. With co-author, Thomas O'Neil, he published *Cracking Cases: The Science of Solving Crimes* in 2002.

LEEUWENHOEK, Antonie Van (1632-1723)

Dutchman who ran a draper's business in Delft and made lenses as a pastime so that he could take a close look at small, everyday objects. He was possibly influenced by Robert Hooke, the seventeenth century English inventor who published his work in 1665 under the title, *Micrographia*.

Van Leeuwenhoek perfected his single lens microscope in order to view objects at a magnification of more than 200 times. He was the first to discover that hair was more than a simple strand and had an internal structure as well as an outer sheath of scales. He is also credited with the discovery of bacteria, which he described in 1683, and opened up new vistas of exploration with his descriptions of blood corpuscles and spermatozoa.

The wonders of discovery made possible by looking through a single lens were magnified beyond imagination when a second lens was used to enhance the first and create a compound microscope. This revolutionised the way human beings saw their world and triggered off the new science of microscopy with its many applications in forensic work.

Van Leeuwenhoek was elected a Fellow of the Royal Society in 1680 and joined leading members such as Robert Hooke and Sir Christopher Wren.

LOCARD, Dr. Edmond (1877-1966)

If forensic science has a founding father, by popular acclaim, that person would almost certainly be Locard. He is one of the great names in criminology and crime investigation. He articulated one of the basic tenets of forensic science which is that every contact leaves a trace, sometimes referred to as "Locard's Principle".

He was an admirer of Sir Arthur Conan **Doyle**, whose fictional detective, Sherlock Holmes, was also a pioneer when it came to assessing a crime scene. The two men met in 1921 when Conan Doyle visited Lyon where Locard had set up his laboratory.

Locard graduated in medicine and the law at the University of Lyon and studied under both **Bertillon** and **Lacassagne**. He travelled widely in Europe and the USA to visit centres of forensic learning and he set his sights on bringing all the scientific disciplines together to further the investigation of crime. Influenced by Hans **Gross**, he also began to talk about police science.

In 1912, he became involved in a murder case which gripped the whole of France and, through his efforts, brought forensic science to the attention of the public. A young woman had been found dead from strangulation and suspicion fell on her fiancé who appeared to have a convincing alibi. Locard took scrapings from beneath the man's fingernails which he viewed under a microscope. He found traces of distinctive particles which he matched to the specially made make-up used by the dead woman. The man confessed to his crime and provided the perfect demonstration of the principle that every contact leaves a trace.

During World War One, Locard extended his range of studies by becoming involved in graphology and cipher work for the French government. In a long career he had taken on the roles of researcher and teacher, bringing innovation to both. He founded the Institute of Criminalistics at Lyon and was appointed its first Director.

Among his many achievements was a seven volume *Traité de*

Criminalistique, started in 1912 and completed over two decades later. It was a fitting testimony to his dedication and life's work.

LOMBROSO, Cesare
(1835-1909)

Regarded by some as the father of criminology, Lombroso's achievement was to use science as a means of understanding the criminal personality. After serving as an army surgeon in his native Italy, he came Professor of Psychiatry at Padua. He made visits to the lunatic asylum at Pesaro to study at first hand possible links between behaviour and physical appearance.

He dissected the brains of human cadavers and examined the inmates of numerous prisons looking for distinguishing characteristics. His conclusion was that there was a category of born criminals, individuals who had reverted to a primitive type. Based on studies of thousands of criminals, Lombroso believed the born criminal was distinguished by physical characteristics such as facial asymmetry, large head and jaws, long arms and low stature. These were, he believed, the stigmata of criminality.

In 1876, Lombroso published his findings in *L'Uomo deliquente* (criminal man). He used body measurements to codify various criminal types such as murderers, rapists and thieves. In the same year, he was appointed Professor of Psychiatry at Turin and later, Professor of Criminal Anthropology.

While Lombroso's theories were not supported by independent scientific research and became discredited, he is recognised for shifting the focus of interest from the crime itself and towards its perpetrator. He thereby opened a new field of study, forensic anthropology. Critics in 1913 repudiated his concept of the physical criminal type following statistical studies carried out on thousands of prison inmates. In 1899, Lombroso published, *Crime: Causes and Remedies*, in which he set out his ideas that the criminal is a different physical type to the non-criminal.

LUCAS, Dr. Alfred (1867-1945)

One of the foremost authorities on forensic chemistry who believed that virtually every activity in life involves some sort of chemistry. He resisted the notion that forensic chemistry should be drawn into the orbit of medical jurisprudence, on the grounds that the subject's boundaries were very wide and ill-defined. He described his work as "chemistry exercised in the service of the law".

During World War One, Lucas worked as a chemist in the Egyptian Government Analytical Laboratory in Cairo. In a varied career, he applied his specialist skills to everything from document examination, forensic ballistics and analysis of hair, fibres and dust. He also made a study of the chemical composition of different kinds of tobacco ash in an echo of Sherlock Holmes's famous monograph on the subject.

In 1921, he published *Forensic Chemistry and Scientific Criminal Investigation* which went to many editions. In the preface to the 1945 edition he mentioned "a few miscellaneous cases" which included the erasure of inscriptions from rubber tyres; an unusual forensic assignment.

Lucas demonstrated amazing breadth and versatility in his work which bore out his belief that everything that is inert or living has a chemical basis.

LYNCH, Dr. Gerald Roche (1889-1957)

Acknowledged as a pioneer in scientific criminology, Dr. Lynch was appointed a junior analyst at the Home Office following his service in the navy during World War One. Later, he became Director of Pathological Chemistry at St. Mary's Hospital, London, where he worked closely with Sir Bernard **Spilsbury** and Sir William **Willcox**.

He was a specialist in toxicology and blood testing and he featured in a controversial case in 1939 when the body of an eleven year old girl was found in fields in Sussex. She had been strangled and sexually assaulted. A cigarette butt found near the body was thought to have been dropped by her attacker. In the absence of any other trace evidence, attention focussed on the cigarette and the possibility of testing for saliva and indications of blood grouping.

This task fell to Dr. Lynch and he quickly established that saliva traces had been made by a non-secreter. This meant that he belonged to the 14% of the population whose body fluids did not give indications of blood groups. The man suspected of committing the crime was sent to trial but was found not guilty of murder.

This was a disappointing outcome for the first, attempt in England to determine blood grouping from saliva. But, as forensic serology continued to edge forward, researchers narrowed the chances of criminals getting away with their crimes and the discovery of DNA in the 1950s provided a major breakthrough.

Dr. Lynch brought his forensic skills to bear on many famous cases and he regularly published his work. To a degree, he worked under the shadow of Sir William Willcox as Senior Home Office Analyst in 1920, a post he held for thirty-four years.

MacDONELL, Dr. Herbert Leon (1928-)

American criminologist who made a special study of blood spatter analysis. He examined spatter patterns at violent crime scenes to determine the direction of blows delivered in blunt force trauma and the likely instrument used. He also looked at the dynamics of airborne blood droplets and the angles at which they strike different surfaces. The examination of blood spatter became a new procedure helping investigators to re-construct a crime scene.

In 1971, MacDonell published what was widely regarded as the standard textbook in his field, *Flight Characteristics and Stain Patterns of Human Blood*. Fellow criminologist, Dr. Paul Leland **Kirk**, did much to establish the value of this kind of analysis in his work on the Marilyn Sheppard case in 1954.

MacDonell's masterly reconstruction of the murder scene in the Zeigler case in 1975 helped to ensure a conviction. Four people were shot dead and one wounded in an attack at a furniture store in Orange County, Florida. After a lengthy examination of the crime scene, MacDonell cross-referenced every detail which included blood spatter, spray patterns, blood trails and footprints where bodies had been moved by the killer who used two firearms and a bludgeon. In a forthright courtroom reconstruction of the crime scene, he showed that Tommy Zeigler had killed four times before wounding himself.

The result bore out MacDonell's philosophy which was that the evidence never lies which he used as the title of his book published in 1984. He served as Director of Forensic Science at Corning, New York State and contributed to many high profile police investigations, including that of O.J. Simpson in 1994.

MACÉ, Gustave (1835-1904)

Celebrated nineteenth-century French detective who became the head of the Sûreté in 1879. He was particularly noted for solving the Voirbo case employing a combination of instinct and logic. Solving the murder case was an early example of systematic crime scene investigation.

When a Parisian restaurateur became aware that the well supplying his water was emitting a foul smell, he investigated the cause. When this turned out to be due to a dismembered limb, he called the police and acquired the services of Monsieur Macé. On further investigation, another limb was found in the well.

As a result of his enquiries, Macé's suspicion fell on a man called Pierre Voirbo who did odd jobs, including collection of well water for nearby residents. When he searched Voirbo's rooms, the detective found items belonging to a man named Bodasse who had been reported missing. Surveying the room, Macé became convinced that Voirbo had dismembered him on the table.

Following his instincts, Macé knew that blood from a messy dismemberment would have dripped onto the tiled floor and later been cleaned up. He noticed there was a slight dip in the tiled surface and, without hesitation, poured a jug of water onto the floor to see where it flowed. As he expected, it collected in the dip and, prising up some of the tiles, he found caked blood beneath. Voirbo made a confession to murder.

Macé gave a graphic account of the Voirbo case in his book of memoirs, *My First Crime*, published in 1886. He noted his thought process at the time when he realised that water would follow the same course as the blood. "When it stops", he wrote, "we will find evidence of the crime".

MALPIGHI, Marcello (1628-1694)

One of the great scientists of the seventeenth century and a pioneer in the use of the microscope. He made many important discoveries which aided understanding of animal and plant life.

Malpighi qualified in Medicine at the University of Bolgna in Italy and spent his life teaching and carrying out research there and at Pisa. In 1661, he described the part played by capillaries in circulating the blood. He took the study of microscopic anatomy to new levels and discovered structures in the kidney and spleen which bear his name.

Among his many projects was that of embryology and viewing the growth of chick eggs under the microscope. Of significance to later scientific developments was Malpighi's description of ridge patterns on the fingers. His observations pointed the way to the subsequent use of fingerprints as a means of identification. The structure which lies beneath the epidermis of the skin is known to anatomists as the *Stratum Malpighi*.

Like his contemporary, Van **Leeuwenhoek** in the Netherlands, Malpighi was honoured by the Royal Society in London for his pioneering research. Three years before his death, in recognition of his immense status in Italy, he was appointed physician to the Pope.

MAPLES, Dr. William R. (1937-1997)

Forensic anthropologist and curator of the Human Identification Laboratory at the Florida Museum of Natural History in the USA.

This facility is used as a teaching centre and also as a base for crime scene investigation work.

Dr. Maples's skill in identifying human remains has earned him an international reputation. In 1992, he was invited by the Russian authorities to examine the recently discovered remains thought to be those of the Romanoff family massacred at Ekaterinburg in 1918.

Five female and four male skeletons came under his scrutiny. By examining the bones and dentition, Dr. Maples and his team, identified the remains of the Czar and Czarina, three of their children and four servants. Czar Nicholas's son, Alexei, and eldest daughter, Anastasia, were unaccounted for.

The physical identification of the Romanoff remains was confirmed in 1993 by matching DNA with a sample provided by the British Royal Family with a bloodline going back to Queen Victoria and shared by her European relatives.

Dr. Maples published a memoir in 1994, *Dead Men Do Tell Tales*, co-written with Michael Browning. He served as President of the American Board of Forensic Anthropology and is a fellow of the American Academy of Forensic Sciences.

MARSH, James (1794-1846)

A chemist who spent his entire working life at the Royal Arsenal in Woolwich, London. In the course of his work, he found a reference to the Swedish chemist, Karl **Scheele**, explaining how he had manufactured arsine gas from white arsenic. This discovery, made in 1775, struck a cord with Marsh who had been following a murder trial involving an accusation of arsenic poisoning. The suspect was acquitted because the presence of arsenic in the corpse could not be proved.

Inspired by his discovery of Scheele's work, Marsh began to experiment with methods to detect arsenic. He found that by mixing a mineral acid with any fluid containing arsenic and then adding zinc to generate hydrogen, a chemical reaction resulted which produced arsine gas. By applying heat, he found that traces of arsenic in the gas were deposited as a metallic mirror in a glass tube. What became known as the Marsh test was the breakthrough that toxicologists had been waiting for. It proved to be reliable and could detect small quantities of arsenic.

James Marsh published his findings in 1836 in *The Edinburgh New Philosophical Journal*, using the simple title, "The Test for Arsenic". His discovery caused ripples of excitement throughout Europe and, not least, in Paris in 1840, which was gripped with the drama of the Marie Lafarge poisoning case. Using the Marsh test, Mathieu **Orfila**, regarded by many as the father of toxicology, detected the presence of arsenic in the victim's organs. Marsh could hardly have wished for a more conclusive endorsement of his work.

In due course, the test was refined and became the Marsh-Berzelius Process in 1906. This made it easier to use and increased its sensitivity. Quicker and more refined tests would evolve using absorption spectroscopy and X-ray fluorescence spectroscopy.

MÉGNIN, Jean Pierre (1828-1905)

French military veterinarian who studied the part that insect activity on a corpse played in helping to determine time of death (TOD). His speciality was animal skin diseases and the treatment of dogs for parasitic mites. It was in the latter capacity that Dr. Mégnin was consulted in 1878, when the semi-mummified corpse of a child was found to be infested with small spiders. He analysed this insect activity and determined that the baby had died at least six months before discovery.

This involvement with the world of forensic detection, convinced Mégnin that his expertise could help to open up a new scientific approach to crime resolution. He began research on the life cycle of blowflies and saw that such activity could provide surprisingly accurate indicators of the post mortem interval. In 1894, he published *La Faune des Cadavres* and forensic entomology was put on the map.

Some of Mégnin's fellow scientists did not believe his work was to be taken seriously. That view did not prevail in the world of legal medicine, though, where the potential of his research was welcomed. He extended his studies to include all the variables that affected insect populations on a corpse, including whether or not the body was buried or left exposed in the open, the time of year, ground conditions, temperature and much more.

He was appointed Professor of Zoology at the School of Veterinary Medicine at Vincennes where he consolidated his life's work. By the time of his death, the principle that post mortem interval could be determined by analysing the insect life present on a decomposing body was well established.

McDONALD, Hugh C.

While working in Europe in the aftermath of World War Two helping the occupation forces to pursue black marketeers and fraudsters, McDonald devised a novel method for identifying suspects. Drawing on the concept of portrait parlé, a speaking likeness, pioneered in the 1890's by **Bertillon**, he came up with the Identikit concept.

Witnesses' descriptions of crime suspects were usually hazy, unreliable and, frequently, time wasting. To facilitate the process McDonald drew sketches of different face shapes and features such as eyes, noses and hairlines, so that a composite face could be assembled from remembered details.

Returning to the USA and his work with the Los Angeles Police Department, McDonald set out to found a company that would develop his idea for use by law enforcement agencies. Identikit thereby became established as the first practical identification system which its inventor claimed could be used to construct sixty-two billion different faces.

Identikit incorporated over five hundred numbered facial features, although, paradoxically, these did not include ears. Although ears were regarded as an important identifying feature by nineteenth-century innovators, it was not included in Identikit on the grounds that most witnesses when they looked at a suspect did so from a full-face perspective.

Identikit was in global use by 1960 and its easy-to-use composite formula meant that a coded face could be transmitted between police forces and between countries. The system dominated police identification procedures for many years before being superseded in 1970 by Photofit and in 1988 by E-FIT.

MITCHELL, Charles Ainsworth (1867-1948)

Noted chemist and analyst whose special field was document examination and, in particular, the chemistry of inks and paper.

He published widely and his contributions to the scientific journals speak for the diversity of his talents, including detection of fingerprints on documents, estimating the age of inked writing, the deciphering of partially destroyed documents and sequences of pen strokes.

He thought of himself as a scientific detective and paid tribute to Edgar Allan Poe as the originator of the modern detective. Mitchell frequently gave evidence in court cases and he made a breakthrough discovery in the case of the Southampton Garage murder in 1929.

The body of an oil company agent was found in a locked garage. He had been bludgeoned to death with a hammer. A scrap of grease-stained paper found at the scene provided a vital clue. Writing on the paper was obscured by dirt and oil but Mitchell cleaned the piece of paper with benzene and salvaged the pencilled writing on it using oblique lighting and photography. This scrap of salvaged evidence led to the identification of the murderer as William Podmore.

Mitchell served as editor of *The Analyst* journal for twenty-five years and Secretary of the Society of Public Analysts for twelve. He also served a term as President of the Medico-Legal Society in 1935 and is acknowledged as a leader in the application of scientific methods to the examination of documents.

NEAVE, Richard A.H. (1936-)

Medical illustrator in the Department of Anatomy at Manchester University Medical School specialising in the reconstruction of heads and faces when normal recognition has been prevented by age or damage. He played a major role in reconstructing the appearance of Egyptian mummies during a university investigation in 1975. His work has also proved crucial in helping the police to identify the skeletal remains of long dead victims of crime.

The process, developed in the 1920s by Mikhail **Gerasimov**, involves making a cast of the skull and building up the muscles using modelling clay. This relies on a correlation between the skull and muscle thickness in different areas.

In December 1993, a partially burned headless corpse was found in Manchester. Identity remained a mystery until a severed head turned up in a shallow grave over seventy miles away. DNA testing proved that the head belonged to the torso but identity remained to be established.

At this point, Richard Neave entered the investigation and proved successful in reconstructing a man's head and face from the smashed remains of the skull. The lifelike reconstruction was photographed by the police and the image was published by the media. Identification came very quickly from a person who had known the dead man, a Kuwaiti business entrepreneur, who had become a murder victim.

NEUSTATTER, Dr. W. Lindesay (1904-1979)

Forensic psychiatrist and consultant at the Royal Northern Hospital in London. He raised the profile of forensic psychiatry with his efforts to understand the criminal mind. He believed that doctors often confused responsibility, that is the extent to which a person is accountable for their acts, with culpability, which signifies the degree of intention.

Neustatter brought new thinking to bear on a range of mental disorders. His view was that emphasising motive reveals little about a criminal's psychology unless it is accompanied by a full background history.

In his book, *The Mind of the Murderer*, published in 1957, he explored different categories of murder according to background psychological disorders, such as schizophrenia, paranoia, sadism and hysteria. Using these assessments, Dr. Neustatter classed John Haigh, the Acid Bath Murderer, as a simulator of insanity and Neville Heath, as a psychopathic sadist.

His publications also included *Psychological Disorder and Crime* (1953) and *Modern Psychiatry in Practice* (1948). He also served as Vice-President of the Medico-Legal Society.

NORRIS, Dr. Charles (1867-1935)

New York City's first medical examiner, appointed in 1918, who is credited with establishing a model system for forensic pathology. Norris's thinking was influenced by his early studies in Europe and encounters with leading forensic investigators of the time.

Dr. Norris had a reputation for expressing independent views and adopted a single-minded approach to medico-legal work. In 1920, Joseph Bowne Elwell, a renowned bridge player, was found dead in his New York apartment with a single gunshot injury to the head. His death was described as suicide, but Norris disagreed. He argued that the position of the wound ruled out a self-inflicted wound and pointed to murder. The original verdict was thereby overturned. The case remained a cause célèbre among unsolved murders.

Further homicide cases in New York raised the profile of forensic investigation to the point where New York Medical School established the first Department of Forensic Medicine in the USA in 1932. Dr. Norris was appointed professor in recognition of his pioneering achievements.

He made a habit of overturning seemingly open and shut cases including that of Francesco Travia who in 1926, confessed to murdering a woman and dismembering her corpse for disposal. The dead woman's torso was found in Travia's apartment and, from its discolouration, Dr. Norris determined that she had died from carbon monoxide poisoning due to a faulty stove and had not been murdered. Travia was acquitted.

NORRIS, Dr. Joel

Foremost authority on the psychology of serial killers. In 1984, the FBI stated that the USA was in the grip of an epidemic of serial murder. This prompted Dr. Norris to make a study of episodic aggression which included interviews with known serial killers.

He found a number of factors which stimulated certain individuals to commit violence on a serial basis. Triggers for violent behaviour included social deprivation, childhood trauma, lack of achievement and low self-esteem. In combination, social, biochemical and psychological factors lay at the core of episodic aggressive outbursts. Dr. Norris described serial murder as a form of disease which needed to be identified and diagnosed in order to protect the public.

His book, *Serial Killers*, published in 1990, included an analysis of deviant behaviour and he listed physical abnormalities that were outward signs of genetic disorders. They represented an anthropometric dimension which might make it possible to identify individuals susceptible to violent behaviour.

Dr. Norris followed this work with *The Killer Next Door*, published in 1992 in which he detailed his studies of seven serial killers. His analysis showed how each individual gave warning signs of likely violence which were not recognised at the time by those with whom they lived and worked. His aim was to establish the criteria whereby what he termed "potential dangerousness" can be measured and acted upon by employers and health care professionals. He also helped to set up the International Committee of Neuroscientists to Study Episodic Aggression.

ORFILA, Mathieu Joseph Bonavente (1787-1853)

One of the great men of forensic science and widely regarded as the founding father of toxicology. He qualified in medicine at Paris in 1811 but his real interests lay in chemistry.

Fascinated by poisons, Orfila set up his own laboratory at home so that he could work long hours without interruption. In 1813, he published the first volume of his celebrated *Traité des Poisons*, which represented the sum of all knowledge on the subject at that time. In 1819, he was appointed Professor of Chemistry at the University of Paris and, subsequently, Professor of Medical Jurisprudence.

He enjoyed an immense reputation throughout Europe and his success attracted aspiring chemists and doctors to Paris to study his methods. Among those inspired by his teaching was Jean **Stas** who, in due course, made his own contribution to the study of toxicology.

In 1840, Orfila was called on to help resolve one of France's most famous poison cases, that of Marie Lafarge, accused of killing her husband with arsenic. Initially, he advised the defence which successfully challenged the inept way in which the toxicology tests had been carried out using out-moded methods. Further tests were commissioned using the new method pioneered by James **Marsh** which gave negative results.

There was jubilation in the Lafarge camp when Marie was found innocent. This was short-lived before Orfila questioned the competence of those conducting the new test. He meticulously carried out further tests which clearly showed the presence of arsenic in the body of Lafarge's husband. She was, accordingly, found guilty and Orfila's reputation took a leap forward. He went on to acquire honours from both academia and the French nation.

OSBORN, Albert Sherman (1858-1946)

American graphologist who dominated the field in a long career and provided expert testimony in a number of high profile court cases. He devised a method of analysing disputed signatures on documents by photographing them under a glass plate ruled with a grid. By this means, he could compare known and suspect signatures and detect forgeries. The working principle was that no two signatures are absolutely identical. Consequently, where a forger slavishly traced a signature for transfer to a fraudulent document, he gave himself away.

Osborn applied similar methods to the examination of suspect typewritten material. By photographing a typed text under his grid, he could identify inequalities in spacing and alignment that were as unique as a fingerprint. He believed it was possible to identify an individual typewriter by its singular characteristics in much the same way that a firearm can be identified.

In 1932, he was called upon to assist the investigation into the kidnapping of the Lindbergh baby. The kidnapper had sent numerous ransom notes which Osborn concluded had been handwritten by a writer of German origin. When Bruno Hauptmann was apprehended, he submitted writing which, in spelling and phraseology, corresponded with that of the ransom notes. In due course, the former soldier in the German army was found guilty of kidnap and murder.

Osborn's two books, *Questioned Documents*, published in 1910, and *The Problem of Proof*, in 1922, became standard textbooks in the field of document examination.

OTTOLENGHI, Professor Salvatore (1861-1934)

He set up the Scuola di Polizia Scientifica at the University of Rome in 1932. It became one of the most respected institutions in Europe devoted to criminal identification.

Influenced by **Bertillon**'s anthropometric methods, he developed and applied the process of portrait parlé (speaking likeness). He moved with the times, though, and when fingerprints superseded Bertillonage he readily accepted the advantages.

PARÉ, Dr. Ambroise (1510-1590)

Prompted by the work of Andreas **Vesalius** in mapping human anatomy, Paré began to investigate the effects of violence on the body. He gained experience treating battle casualties, particularly gunshot wounds, and initiated a number of surgical procedures which saved lives. In 1545, he published a book on methods of curing wounds, including applying ligatures to damaged arteries in place of cauterisation.

He was highly regarded as a surgeon to the extent that he was appointed to serve four French kings. He was certainly a pioneer and viewed historically as the father of forensic medicine. He published many articles, including a treatise on procedures for compiling medical reports.

PEARSON, Professor Karl (1857-1936)

Mathematician with a wide range of interests who was appointed Professor of Applied Mathematics and Mechanics at University College London. He developed an interest in biometry and evolutionary theory and established a biometric laboratory intended to solve scientific problems using mathematics.

He devised a method for estimating the height of a human body by measuring the long bones in the skeleton and applying a mathematical formula. He also formulated a method for determining the sex of the human frame using a mathematical formula based on measurements of the heads of the humerous and femur.

"Pearson's Formula" for estimating stature, devised in 1899, was confirmed in a set of tables which, though not a precise guide, offered valuable approximations of height, especially where only partial skeletal remains were available.

He published a *Study of the long bones of the English Skeleton Part 1, The Femur*, in 1919.

PENRY, Jacques

Inventor of the Photofit system of facial identification which superceded Identikit in 1970. Penry, who described himself as a facial photographer, developed his interest in faces while working in Canada in the 1930s.

He noted that "we are all potential witnesses to crime", and stressed the importance of witnesses' recollection of a suspect. He started by defining basic facial shape and associated features and recording them as photographs. These interchangeable components could then be built up to create a composite likeness, called a photofit. The advantage of this approach was that it had a realism which Identikit lacked.

Returning to work in the UK, including a spell as a quick-sketch artist on television, he interested the Home Office in his invention and trials were successfully completed. Penry's early Photofit kits offered over twelve billion permutations and, in 1970, his system was officially adopted for use by British police forces.

Introduction of the system was not straightforward and Penry and the Home Office disagreed about the way it should be developed. Furthermore, police officers expressed some reservations about its effectiveness in identifying suspects.

Disenchanted by the lack of progress in Britain, Penry moved to the USA in 1977. This too proved less than satisfactory due to contractual difficulties over the manufacture of Photofit Kits. In

1988, Photofit was overtaken by a computerised identification system called E-FIT.

PEREIRA, Dr. Margaret (1928-2016)

Trained as a chemist and worked for twenty-nine years at the Metropolitan Police Laboratory in London. Her work on blood grouping was recognised worldwide and she took the identification of bloodstains to new levels of accuracy.

Dr. Pereira developed methods enabling the analysis of multiple blood samples to be tested for particular constituents. She rationalised standard test procedures making them more user-friendly and constantly refined serological techniques.

She left Scotland Yard's police laboratory in 1976 to join the Home Office Forensic Science Service and became controller of the Service in 1982. She was widely acknowledged for her dedication to the challenges confronted by serologists in their search for fast and accurate methods of analysing crime scene blood evidence.

POLLER, Dr. Alphonse

Austrian criminologist who developed techniques for taking casts of three-dimensional objects. He used resinous compounds to make vividly accurate moulage reproductions of heads, hands and feet. He made a reference collection of hands to demonstrate the marks and calluses made by various crafts. These were the occupational marks acquired by bakers, cobblers and tailors, among others, using the tools of their particular trade.

By examining a crime suspect's hands, a trained police officer could determine his likely occupation or trade. Dr. Poller's casts were made from a moulage consisting of a hydro-colloidal compound which moulded fine detail. It could be safely used to make casts directly from a suspect's body.

The Vienna Police Department kept a collection of Poller's casts which were used for training and reference purposes.

POPP, Dr. Georg (1861-1943)

German commercial chemist based in Frankfurt where he ran his own company offering science-based applications for agriculture and the food industry. He developed an interest in crime investigation having studied the teachings of **Gross** and **Bertillon**.

In 1904, he helped to solve a murder case which involved the transfer of soil from the crime scene to the clothing of the suspect. Using microscopical methods, and his knowledge of soil characteristics, Popp showed there was a match. As a result, the man who strangled a young girl in a field was convicted of her murder. Solving this high profile case made Popp a forensic celebrity and his work was hailed by one newspaper as "The Microscope as Detective".

In lectures to learned societies, Dr. Popp stressed the prominent part that chemistry, mineralogy and botany could play in the investigation of crime. He set up a museum in which he displayed photomicrographs related to cases he had worked on and encouraged a generation of budding criminologists. He made examination of soil trace evidence a forensic discipline with an emphasis on geology.

PURKINJE, Johann Evangelista (1787-1869)

Czechoslovakian physiologist at the University of Breslau who, in 1823, made a systematic description of the ridges and furrows on the skin surfaces of the hands and feet. His thesis, referring to nine different fingerprint patterns, including spirals, loops and whorls, was the foundation of modern fingerprint identification.

Purkinje qualified in medicine at the University of Prague in 1819 and returned thirty-one years later as Professor of Physiology and Pathology. He is credited with many discoveries relating to the function of the eye and he pioneered the microscopic examination of tissues thinly sliced on a microtome. This was the beginning of histology as a means of studying anatomy at the cellular level. It was also an important advance in teaching methods.

An outstanding practitioner of experimental physiology, Purkinje was a strong advocate of laboratory-based procedures. His description of fingerprint patterns was a landmark in the developing science of personal identification at a time when other scientists were waiting in the wings to build on his work.

QUETELET, Lambert Adolphe Jacques (1796-1874)

Belgian statistician and astronomer whose work provided a basis for developments in personal identification. Widely regarded as the father of modern statistics, he set out to establish a scientific basis for human individuality. He believed that everything in the natural world showed unlimited and infinite variation in form.

Applying this principle, Quetelet concluded that no two human beings could be totally identical in their physical measurements. He collected measurement statistics which bore out his theory and led to the possibility of using their unique body measurements to identify criminals. In 1835, he published *A Treatise On Man and the Development of his Faculties*. An early example of his ideas put into practice was reported to be the measurement of inmates at Louvain Prison in 1860.

In time, Quetelet's concept of the uniqueness of each individual was taken up by Alphonse **Bertillon** and incorporated in his system of anthropometry as a means of recording the identity of criminals. In turn, this led to another facet of uniqueness which was the human fingerprint.

Quetelet became Director of the Royal Observatory in Brussels and he organised the first international congress on statistics in 1853. Three years before his death, he published his work under the title, *Anthropometry, or the Measurement of Different Faculties of Man*. While he came to be regarded as the founder of statistics, he is honoured in the forensic world as a pathfinder in criminal identification.

REISS, Dr. Rudolph Archibald (1875-1929)

Born in Germany but a naturalised Swiss citizen, Reiss was appointed Professor of Police Science at Lausanne University in

1906. His early interest in photography was crucial to his later work when he pioneered the use of the camera to record crime scene evidence in situ.

Reiss taught forensic photography at Lausanne and made the Institute of Police Science a leader in the rapidly evolving world of criminology and criminalistics. He was an accomplished teacher and helped police agencies in many countries to develop their own laboratory-based crime scene investigations.

His legacy is the institute which he founded in Lausanne that has taught generations of young forensic scientists since the beginning of the twentieth century. Reiss's special contribution was a study of forged fingerprints. In 1911, he published a comprehensive *Manual of Police Science*.

He was particularly drawn to Serbia where he worked for several years in the former Yugoslavia where he died in 1929.

SCHEELE, Karl Wilhelm
(1742-1786)

Swedish chemist who probably did not achieve the credit he deserved in his lifetime for many of his discoveries. He identified oxygen and chlorine before their acknowledged discoveries and also found a number of new chemical elements, including manganese, barium and tungsten.

His innovations included a method for manufacturing arsine gas from white arsenic which led to the first reliable method of identifying the element in crime investigation (see James **Marsh**). In 1775, he devised a method of detecting arsenic in corpses. It was still not possible at this stage to trace small doses but his method enabled large doses to be detected. He inspired others to follow his investigative methods, including **Orfila** and Marsh, which led to the emergence of toxicology.

Scheele trained as an apprentice pharmacist and commanded his subject with such inventive flair that he was elected to the Swedish Royal Academy of Sciences. He died at the early age of forty-three, possibly due to poor health resulting from a lifetime's exposure to toxic chemicals which included research on manufacturing phosphorus.

SCHIFF, Fritz (1889-1940)

German scientists were in the vanguard in developing forensic serology in the early 1900s by refining and extending the work of fellow scientists in other countries. In 1923, a Japanese researcher at Hokkaido University showed that the body fluids of 80% of human individuals possessed the same group characteristics as their blood. Experimenting initially with saliva and semen, Dr. Yamakami went on to demonstrate that this characteristic extended to all body fluids, including urine, sweat and even mother's milk.

This development had enormous significance for forensic science and Dr. Schiff, working in Berlin on testing methods to establish paternity, realised its potential. In 1932, he defined the two groups identified by Yamakami as secretors (86%) and non-secretors (14%).

The implication of this work was that the blood group of a person who had sweated into a piece of clothing, licked the flap on an envelope, discarded a cigarette butt or deposited a semen stain on a bed sheet could be determined. Crime scientists in many countries were soon reporting successes using the new blood grouping techniques. The impact of these developments was only modified by the knowledge that the 14% of the human population who were non-secretors, passed through the forensic net.

Schiff published his work on the *Medico-Legal Significance of Blood Groups* in 1929 and, six years later, emigrated to the USA to escape the rising influence of Nazism. He continued his work there as an enterprising serologist and bacteriologist until his death in 1940.

SELMI, Francesco (1817-1881)

Italian chemist who studied the process of putrefaction and discovered that certain alkaloids form naturally in dead bodies and may be misinterpreted as poisons deliberately administered with intent to kill. Selmi's discovery of cadaveric alkaloids highlighted the possibility that a person might be wrongfully accused of committing murder by poison.

In two high profile poison cases in Italy, Selmi showed that cadaveric alkaloids were mistaken for deliberately administered poison. His findings helped to prevent the possibility of miscarriages of justice and the Italian government was sufficiently concerned by the turn of events to set up a special scientific commission to look into the toxicological problems involved.

Selmi became Professor of Pharmaceutical Chemistry at the University of Bologna and, in 1878, published his work in a paper in which he coined the term, ptomaine poisoning. This dealt with the science of poisonous alkaloids formed by bacterial action on putrefying remains.

While the boundaries of toxicology had been pushed back, Selmi's work provided nimble lawyers with a weapon to defend clients accused of murder by poisoning. One such case was that of Dr. George Lamson, tried in London in 1882 on a charge of using aconite to kill his brother-in-law. The question of cadaveric alkaloids being mistaken for deliberately administered poison was raised by the defence. The attempt was defeated and Lamson was duly convicted of a crime for which he later confessed.

SIMPSON, Professor Keith (1907-1985)

After qualification, Dr. Simpson decided to specialise in pathology and, in 1932, was appointed demonstrator at Guy's Hospital Medical School. A contemporary of **Spilsbury** and **Camps**, he was an innovator as well as a practitioner and teacher.

He featured in several high-profile murder investigations and, notably, that of John Haigh, the infamous Acid Bath Murderer, in 1949. A suspect from the very beginning when a lady acquaintance went missing, Haigh boasted that it was not possible to bring a murder charge when there was no body.

Simpson proved him wrong when the pathologist's intuition told him that a lady of the missing woman's age might have suffered with gallstones. When he scrutinised the sludge emptied from one of Haigh's acid drums, he found several gallstones which proved the remains were human, and a denture, which enabled him to confirm the identity of the murder victim.

Simpson was a pioneer of forensic dentistry and he introduced this dimension to a number of investigations, including the Hay case in 1967. He showed that bite marks made on the victim's body matched the dentition of the chief suspect.

He wrote a highly successful textbook, *Forensic Medicine*, in 1947 which went to several editions. In 1961, he was elected President of the Medico-Legal Society and, in the following year, was appointed Professor of Forensic Medicine at London University. Simpson was regarded as an outstanding lecturer and won many plaudits for his teaching skills. In 1978, he published his autobiography, *Forty Years of Murder*, which charted the highlights of an outstanding career.

SMITH, Sir Sydney (1883-1969)

Widely travelled New Zealander who exercised his skills as a forensic pathologist in many parts of the world. He spent the early part of his career in Egypt where he developed the emerging science of forensic ballistics and retired in Edinburgh where he served as Professor of Forensic Medicine for twenty-five years.

While working in Egypt as Principle Medico-Legal Expert, he developed his skills as a firearms examiner. He adopted procedures pioneered in the USA, particularly use of the comparison microscope to view suspect and test bullets in the same field of vision. He had an early success in 1924 when he identified the weapon used to murder Sir Lee Stack in a Cairo street.

Smith gave expert testimony in a number of high profile murder trials in the UK, including the Ruxton case in 1935, when he worked with fellow Professor, John **Glaister**. He consulted his contemporaries and was always willing to share knowledge and learn from others. He published an authoritative textbook in 1925 entitled, *Forensic Medicine and Toxicology*, in which he noted, "A knowledge of medicine and a stock of common sense are not of themselves sufficient". He emphasised the need to acquire specialised knowledge.

A mark of the esteem in which Sydney Smith was held was that he was invited to take on the editorship of *Taylor's Principles and Practice of Medical Jurisprudence*. First published in 1836, this text was highly regarded and went to many editions down to the present time. In 1959, Professor Smith published an autobiography which he called, *Mostly Murder*.

SÖDERMAN, Dr. Harry (1902-1956)

Leading Scandinavian criminologist recognised as a pioneer in forensic developments. He studied at Lyon University under Dr. Edmond **Locard** and wrote a doctoral thesis on forensic ballistics. In 1927, he published the first spectrographic analysis of powder residues.

In the 1930s, he made what he described as "mundane advances" which included the identification of footprints from both naked feet and also footwear. He made the point that shoe prints are seldom exactly the same size as the shoes that made them. He emphasised that identification is based on wear characteristics, including repairs and the presence of studs. He applied the same thinking to the investigation of vehicle tyre marks found at a crime scene.

In 1931, Dr. Söderman was appointed the first head of the National Laboratory of Forensic Science at the University of Stockholm. He established close links with the New York City Police Department and, in 1935, with John O'Connell of the NYPD as co-author, published *Modern Criminal Investigation*.

The book, with its emphasis on scientifically-based police procedures, was described as a leading manual in its field. Its comprehensive coverage was summarised under the headings, identification of criminals and victims, scene of crime investigation and police laboratory procedures. Dr. Söderman's reputation was such that he was asked by the New York City Police to assist in setting up modern laboratories on their behalf.

SPILSBURY, Sir Bernard (1877-1947)

One of the most celebrated of Britain's forensic pathologists during the first decades of the twentieth century. His fame lay not in his status as a teacher or innovator but as a practitioner and acknowledged expert witness.

He came to prominence in 1910 with his involvement in the famous Crippen murder case. By means of histological examination, he showed that a mark on a piece of skin retrieved from a body buried in a cellar was the result of a surgical operation. This discovery confirmed the identity of the human remains as Crippen's wife. While Dr. Crippen entered the hall of infamy, Spilsbury was rewarded with celebrity status.

Based at St. Mary's Hospital, London, where he had his own laboratory, Spilsbury worked with leading contemporary forensic specialists of the day, including Sir William **Willcox**. After the Crippen case, there followed a succession of high profile murder cases involving practically all known murder methods. The newspapers eagerly pursued these crime investigations and the strap line, "Spilsbury called In", was a mark of the pathologist's celebrity.

Following the loss of his two sons, one killed by enemy action and the other by disease, Spilsbury declined and died by committing suicide in his laboratory at the age of seventy. After his death, it became fashionable to criticise his approach to forensic work and, particularly, his unwillingness, to change his opinions in the face of what others regarded as superior evidence. Certainly, professional demeanour did not allow him to entertain doubts about his own judgement.

STAS, Professor Jean Servais (1813-1891)

Studied medicine and chemistry at the Belgian University of Louvain. He was fascinated by the subject of toxicology and set up a laboratory at his home so that he could pursue his interests more closely. In 1835, he went to Paris where he studied under **Orfila** and, in 1840, he was appointed Professor at the Ecole Royale Militaire in Brussels.

His great contribution to toxicology was the discovery of a means of determining the presence of vegetable poison in human tissues. The method devised by Stas endured for a century and was widely used by laboratories around the world. In 1850, he was called on to help investigators looking into a mysterious death in which a body had been found, stripped and cleaned inside and out with vinegar. There were suspicious that the cleansing was intended to conceal a fatal poisoning. Arsenic was suspected but Stas's findings ruled that out and led to a sensational outcome.

After exhaustive testing, using alcohol and acid to dissolve any alkaloid poisons, Stas identified nicotine as the lethal agent. The investigative trail led to a Belgian nobleman, Count de Bocarmé, who, it appeared, had killed his brother-in-law for gain using nicotine extracted in his cellar laboratory at Tournai.

Stas used newly discovered agents such as ether to perfect his methods and experiments on dogs. A variation of his procedure known as the Stas-Otto process, was widely used for quantitative determination of organic poisons. The measure of Stas's achievement was that the great toxicologist, Orfila, said it could not be done. Stas retired due to ill health in 1869 after over thirty years at the forefront of his profession.

STEVENSON, Sir Thomas
(1838-1908)

Toxicologist and forensic chemist with a distinguished academic background who served as senior scientific analyst at the Home Office from 1881 to 1908.

His breadth of knowledge on poisons used for criminal purposes was second to none and he was frequently called on for advice. His appearances in court as an expert witness brought him to public attention and he testified in numerous high profile trials including those of Maybrick, Cream and Chapman.

He also participated in the trial of Dr. George Lamson in 1881. His contribution to the prosecution case perhaps best exemplified his skills and thoroughness. Lamson was accused of poisoning a relative with aconitine, a little known vegetable poison at that time. His victim was paraplegic and Lamson advised him to take sugar-filled gelatine capsules to counteract the medicine he was prescribed which was foul tasting. The allegation against Lamson was that he had doctored the capsules with aconitine.

The poison is derived from the dried root of Monkshood and was used in proprietary medicine as a cure for neuralgia. It was known that Lamson had bought a quantity of such medicine but the difficulty was proving that he had used it to kill for gain.

The known methods for detecting such alkaloid poisons were primitive and depended on tasting and experiments involving the injection of mice. During his courtroom testimony, Dr. Stevenson gave a painstaking account of how he had made extracts from the victim's internal organs and tasted them for the presence of aconitine, with positive results. He also injected mice with extracts and they quickly succumbed to the poison.

The thoroughness of Stevenson's work in the laboratory was at the edge of what was known about plant poisons and complicated by the knowledge that cadaveric alkaloids produced in a decomposing body had similar characteristics. Stevenson showed to the satisfaction of the court that he could tell the difference. Dr. Lamson was found guilty of murder and subsequently confessed.

Stevenson's knowledge of poisons included arsenic, strychnine, antimony and morphine and his expertise proved compelling in the trials of George Chapman, Dr. Neill Cream and Mrs. Maybrick.

In 1883 he edited and extended Dr. Swaine **Taylor**'s book, *Principles and Practice of Medical Jurisprudence*.

TARDIEU, Dr. Auguste Ambroise (1818-1879)

One of the great figures in forensic medicine during the nineteenth century in France. He made two significant contributions to the development of crime investigation. In 1870, he published a study of death by asphyxia, including hanging, strangulation and suffocation. His description of small effusions of blood (ecchymoses) in the face and on the heart and lungs ensured his enduring fame. "Tardieu spots" achieved diagnostic importance as indicators of congestive asphyxia.

Earlier, in 1849, he published a treatise on the marks made on the body by the pursuit of various occupations. For example, the characteristic callouses on the hands of a shoe-maker marked his working life. Such occupational marks were of significant medico-legal importance in helping to establish personal identification when examining a dead body.

Tardieu contributed to the investigation of a number of famous crimes, including that of Dr. Edmond de la Pommerais in 1863. When de la Pommerais' mistress, whose life he had insured for a large sum, died he certified that she had succumbed to cholera. When suspicions arose, an exhumation was ordered and Tardieu exercised his toxicological skill by analysing body fluids for poison.

Using methods pioneered by Jean **Stas**, his Belgian contemporary, Tardieu injected extracts taken from the dead woman's organs into a dog and observed the effects. The animal exhibited symptoms which he related to those caused by digitalis. It turned out that the doctor had purchased quantities of the drug which he said were used to treat heart disease. The defence at his trial speculated that the poison might have been generated during the process of putrefaction, an argument that raised the subject of cadaveric alkaloids. De la Pommerais was judged guilty of murder.

TAYLOR, Professor Alfred Swaine (1806-1880)

One of the leading British toxicologists of the nineteenth century who featured in many of the great murder trials of the day. He was appointed Professor at Guy's Hospital, London, in 1851 and became a recognised authority on medico-legal matters.

In 1842, he published his *Manual of Medical Jurisprudence*, which went to many editions both in Britain and the USA. In 1845, he was elected a Fellow of the Royal Society.

Taylor is also remembered for an error he made in 1859 in the case of Dr. Smethurst who was charged with killing his wife with arsenic. The toxicologist claimed to have found arsenic in a sample of the dead woman's vomit and testified to that effect at the murder trial. Smethurst was found guilty and sentenced to death, but uncertainties emerged over Taylor's analysis and an enquiry was called for. It emerged that he had inadvertently introduced arsenic in the test sample by using arsenic-tainted chemical reagents.

As a result, Smethurst was reprieved and the standing of both Taylor and forensic science was diminished. In the aftermath, questions were asked about how much faith could be placed in what some were calling "the beastly science".

It took decades for public confidence to be restored which came in the wake of the great murder trials such as that of Dr. Crippen at the beginning of the twentieth century. Professor Taylor's unwitting error was a rare blemish in an otherwise impeccable career. It was a measure of the man that he readily admitted his mistake.

Taylor made an outstanding contribution to the progress of forensic medicine, delivering the first lectures on the subject in England and writing his highly praised *Manual of Medical Jurisprudence*.

TYRRELL, John F. (1861-1955)

For fifty years Tyrrell was a leading document examiner and handwriting expert in the USA. His forte was the identification of handwriting and the associated paper and inks. He could also trace typewritten documents and relate them to a specific machine.

He developed an interest in handwriting as a young man and contributed to *Penman's Art Journal*. A competition run by the magazine was won jointly by Tyrrell and his friend, Albert **Osborn**, who later became an expert in his field.

A particular skill that Tyrrell cultivated was spotting forged signatures on documents handled by insurance companies. He testified in the Rice case in 1902 when Albert Patrick, a corrupt lawyer, was charged with murdering a wealthy client in expectation of benefiting from his death. Tyrrell showed that the signatures on the dead man's will had been forged.

He testified in a number of headline murder cases, including those of Roland Molineux in 1899 and Leopold and Loeb in 1924. In 1932, he played a part in the Lindbergh kidnapping case when he showed that a ransom note demanding $50,000 contained spelling errors which might indicate the author was of German origin. In due course, Bruno Hauptmann was tried for murder and found guilty in a case which remains controversial.

Whether it was forged signatures, ransom letters or fire-damaged documents, Tyrrell, often in association with Albert Osborn, usually found a solution.

UHLENHUTH, Dr. Paul Theodor (1870-1957)

Until 1900 it was not possible to distinguish human from animal blood. Any criminal fleeing a crime scene with blood on his clothes could simply say, without fear of contradiction, that the stains were made by animal blood. Dr. Uhlenhuth changed that by devising a test that made it possible to confirm the source of bloodstains.

After serving as a medic in the German army, Uhlenhuth worked with the renowned scientist, Robert Koch, in Berlin at the Institute for Infectious Diseases. Here he learned about the part that antitoxins played in fighting disease. In 1889, he moved to Greifswald as Assistant Professor carrying out research on the mechanisms whereby the human body defended itself against disease.

Building on the work carried out by Jules Bordet on precipitins, Uhlenhuth experimented with injections of protein from chicken eggs into rabbits. From the animal's blood, he extracted a serum which separated out the protein as a precipitate. Applying this principle more widely, he discovered it was possible to distinguish between animal and human blood.

This was a huge advance in the investigation of blood found at a crime scene and continued research showed that the method could be used to determine the identity of old, dried bloodstains. The precipitin test revolutionised crime laboratory procedures and was quickly adopted by crime scene investigators.

Paul Uhlenhuth continued his researches and made further important discoveries in the field of disease control, immunology and microbiology.

UNDRITZ, Dr. Erik (1901-1984)

German haematologist who worked for a Swiss pharmaceutical company investigating diseases of the blood. By the late 1950s, he was regarded as one of the leading haematologists in Europe.

In 1960, he was asked by the Swiss authorities to assist in the investigation of a murder case. Pierre Jaccoud was accused of killing a man called Zumbach with a knife. A complicating factor was that both victim and suspect were O group blood types. Hence, bloodstains found on the suspect's clothing and a knife believed to be the murder weapon were of little help to investigators. So, other determining factors were needed.

When Dr. Undritz looked at the blood samples under the microscope, he found hitherto unrecognised fragments of tissue which he identified as human liver cells. Here was the connecting evidence linking victim and murderer.

It was conjectured that when the knife used to stab Zumbach was withdrawn from his body, it brought with it cells from his penetrated liver. Further examination of Jaccoud's clothing turned up blood spots containing human liver cells. Using pioneering techniques, Undritz sought to determine both the age and sex of the blood cells. His findings were severely tested at Jaccoud's trial but Undritz's ground-breaking investigation was sufficient to secure a verdict of guilty of manslaughter.

VESALIUS, Andreas (1514-1564)

Flemish anatomist who broke the religious embargo preventing dissection of human corpses. By cutting into and examining the interior of bodies, he made it possible to construct a real picture of their anatomy. In the process, he dispelled many of the myths about how the body was structured and functioned.

His anatomical descriptions were enhanced by outstandingly

detailed illustrations created by the artist, Jan Stephen van Calcar. Their seven volume work, *The Structure of the Human Body*, published in 1543, represented a landmark of knowledge and understanding. Physicians were enabled to raise their awareness of how the body worked and evaluate the effects of illness, injury and disease. A proper knowledge of anatomy was also a foundation for the development of forensic medicine.

Vesalius was not universally praised for his work and was condemned to death by the Inquisition. He escaped this judgement and found protection in the court of Charles V. He travelled a great deal, including visits to Italy where he lectured at learned institutions in Padua and other cities. He died, aged fifty, during a sea voyage in the Mediterranean.

VIDOCQ, Eugène François (1775-1857)

Described as a master of disguise, Vidocq was a man who spent a great deal of his time consorting with criminals in Paris's underworld. As a former convict, he had a rapport with them whereby he gained their confidence while acting as a police spy.

In the early nineteenth century, experienced detectives used sight recognition as a means of identification. By memorising facial characteristics, they could pick out habitual criminals when they re-offended. In 1811, Vidocq became Chief of the Service de Sûreté of Paris and used his skills to the extent that he was praised for the part he played in reducing crime in the city.

He led an adventurous life which he recorded in his *Memoirs of Vidocq*, published in 1928 and, when he left the Sûreté, started a private detective agency. Fortune did not smile on him, though, and he died in poverty.

VOLLMER, August (1876-1955)

Regarded as the father of modern policing in the USA during the time that he served as Chief of Police at Berkeley, California. A former soldier and postal worker, he entered the police service in 1905 and rapidly rose to prominence. He was keen to put policing on a more professional basis and did not hesitate to adopt methods developed in Europe.

Vollmer established a police training unit at the Crime Prevention Bureau in Berkeley in 1908 and acknowledged the work of Hans **Gross**, the Austrian criminologist, in the lectures he gave. He had a reputation as a fearless police officer with a talent for crime solving and a desire to embrace scientific approaches.

His inspired leadership encouraged others to develop new ideas including Leonarde Keeler and John Larson who built and developed the first lie detector in 1921. The prototype was put to use in the questioning of William Hightower over the murder of Father Patrick Heslin in San Francisco. The suspect's answers showed variation in blood pressure consistent with untruthfulness during questioning. Together with other evidence, this confirmed Hightower's guilt.

Vollmer retired in 1932 after a police career lasting twenty-seven years.

VUCETICH, Juan (1858-1925)

Argentinean police official who secured the world's first murder conviction by means of fingerprints found at the crime scene. He joined the police force in Buenos Aires after emigrating from Croatia in 1884.

Vucetich gained rapid promotion and was sent to La Plata to head the police department's identification section using **Bertillon**'s system of anthropometry. Having read about **Galton**'s work on fingerprints, he was inspired to develop his own ten finger classification system. He envisaged that this would supersede anthropometry as a method of identification.

Known as dactyloscopy, his system was soon put to the test. In 1892, a woman was charged in Buenos Aires with murdering her two children. Bloody fingerprints found at the crime scene were matched to the mother using Vucetich's method. As a result, she made a confession to murder.

Vucetich had long abandoned Bertillon's methods and, boosted by his own success, began to develop and improve his system. In 1894, he published his work under the title *Dactiloscopia Comparada*. The Argentine government was so impressed with fingerprint identification that, in 1916, a law was passed requiring the compulsory fingerprinting of all citizens. Vucetich was given the task of implementing the new measures.

All of this proved unacceptable to the public who saw only an erosion of personal freedoms. Such was the outcry that the government overturned the new legislation and ordered all records to be destroyed. Mortified by the turn of events, Vucetich discontinued his researches and went into retirement. As this point, the initiative for developing fingerprinting into a viable system passed back to Europe.

WAITE, Charles E. (1865-1926)

One of the founding fathers of forensic ballistics who was inspired by a miscarriage of justice to seek a scientific basis which enabled bullets to be related to the weapons that fired them.

In 1915, Charles E. Stielow was convicted of a double murder in New York State. On the basis of evidence given by a self-appointed, unqualified 'expert', the court returned a guilty verdict and Stielow faced death in the electric chair. There were misgivings about the evidence and an experienced New York detective was asked to examine the alleged murder weapon. He test-fired the gun and showed that marks on the crime scene bullets could not have been made by that particular gun.

Stielow was reprieved and an innocent man was spared a judicial death. Charles Waite who, at that time, was working in the New York State Prosecutor's Office, decided that the only way to prevent further mistakes was to develop a system to record the characteristics of every type of firearm then available.

After serving with the US Army in World War One, Waite turned his mind to the task he had set himself. He knew that lands and grooves in rifled gun barrels left distinctive marks on bullets fired.

He had also learned that the machine tools used to create the rifling also left unique marks. Waite began to collect information from US gun makers and he built up a reference collection.

Next, he joined forces with Philip O. **Gravelle** and Calvin **Goddard** to form a trio whose insight and innovation made it possible to compare bullets and cartridge cases retrieved from a crime scene and relate them to the weapon which had discharged them. In 1923, Waite and Gravelle founded the Bureau of Forensic Ballistics in New York, the first organisation of its kind. They were later joined by Calvin Goddard.

WALLS, Dr. Hamish J. (1908-1988)

Former Director of the Metropolitan Police Laboratory at Scotland Yard and a pioneering forensic scientist. He was particularly adept in the use of spectrographic analysis to examine trace evidence such as paint fragments.

In 1968, Dr. Walls published an authoritative work, simply called *Forensic Science*. His contemporary Professor Keith **Simpson**, described him as "providing science for the policeman". His involvement as an expert witness in a controversial murder trial in 1962 exemplified his approach to crime scene investigation.

A householder had an altercation with three youths making a noise outside his home. When the trio entered his house uninvited, Colin Chisham produced a .22 rifle and fired two shots, fatally injuring one of them. In his defence Chisham said that, fearing he would be attacked, he fired the gun to warn off the intruders and also struck out with a swordstick.

The question to be answered was whether the fatal wound had been caused by a bullet or by the swordstick. It was a through and through wound with an entry and exit point but no retrievable bullet. Dr. Walls carried out some experiments using a swordstick to pierce the dead youth's jacket to determine the kind of hole it would make.

He found that whereas a bullet left a typical collar of projecting fibres on the inside of the hole, the thrust of a swordstick produced a different effect leaving a few random fibres projecting on the inside of the entry point. Walls, supported by other experts, concluded that the fatal injury had been caused by a bullet and not a blade.

While this evidence supported a charge of murder, on the judge's instructions, the trial jury found the defendant guilty of manslaughter. Dr. Walls was made aware of the disadvantages of an adversarial legal system in the presentation of expert testimony in court. He became an advocate of a system whereby both prosecution and defence had access to one body of forensic evidence provided by the best available laboratory and testing facilities.

In 1972, he published a memoir, entitled *Expert Witness*, in which he set out the details of the Chisham case in a chapter quoting the philosopher, Bernard Russell, and his remark, "Do not feel absolutely certain of anything".

WILLCOX, Sir William
(1870-1941)

Acknowledged as one of the leading figures of his day in the field of forensic investigation in Britain. Initially he studied chemistry but then switched to medicine, qualifying in 1900 at London University. He trained as an analyst under Dr. Thomas **Stevenson** at Guy's Hospital. He was influenced by his mentor to combine toxicological technique with medico-legal applications.

Willcox gave expert testimony in a number of high profile poisoning trials including those of Crippen, Armstrong and Seddon. His particular gift was his willingness to work with and support the pathologists who were his contemporaries, including Sir Bernard **Spilsbury**. This was important, because before the advent of special forensic laboratories, effective investigation especially in poison cases depended on individuals like Willcox working in their own laboratories and sharing information. Willcox was a good performer in court and was reported as saying, "I may look like a fool, but I'm not one".

He served in the army medical corps during World War One and, for a time, was based in Mesopotamia. He worked as a physician dedicated to stemming the loss of life due to infectious disease. From 1919 to 1941, Willcox acted as Honorary Medical Advisor to the Home Office. He was also a sought after lecturer on great crimes and particularly those involving poisoning.

WITTHAUS, Dr. Rudolph August (1846-1915)

American toxicologist who studied chemistry in the USA and France and became Professor of Chemistry at New York University in 1876. He gave expert evidence at a number of murder trials involving morphine poisoning.

In 1892 Carlyle Harris was charged with murder in what proved to be the first conviction for morphine poisoning in New York. Harris, a medical student, had given his young wife capsules of quinine to relieve her insomnia. What emerged later was that he had laced them with morphine. Dr. Witthaus testified at the trial and confirmed that pin-pointed pupils in the eyes were an undeniable indication of morphine poisoning.

In the same year, Witthaus appeared in another high profile poisoning case also involving a doctor and a controversy about pin-pointed pupils. Dr. Robert Buchanan reported the death of his wife in circumstances that led to the exhumation of her body. While morphine poisoning was suspected, the infallible indicator in the eyes was not present. Witnesses came forward to claim that Buchanan had boasted of disguising the effects of morphine by putting belladonna drops in the eyes. That this worked was confirmed in court by experiments carried out by Dr. Witthaus.

The toxicologist published several books on chemistry which were widely read both in the USA and Europe. In particular, his four volume work written with T.C. Becker and published in 1895 was highly praised. It was entitled, *Medical Jurisprudence, Forensic Medicine and Toxicology*.

ZACCHIA, Paolo (1584-1659)

Described by some historians as the "spiritual father of forensic medicine". Zacchia was physician to the Popes of his day and head of the Vatican's medical services. Over a period of thirty years he published nine volumes of forensic studies under the title, *Quaestiones Medico-Legales*. Zacchia developed procedures for examining the victims of violent deaths and relating their wounds to the methods used against them. He drew up protocols to distinguish murder from suicide and studied the effects of different methods such as stabbing and strangulation on the internal organs. By linking medicine to legal inquiries, he established the foundation of medico-legal procedures.

BIBLIOGRAPHY

BADEN, Michael: *Unnatural Death*, London (1951)
BASS, William and JEFFERSON, J.: *Death's Acre*, New York (2003)
BLOCK, Eugene: *Chemist of Crime*, London (1959)
BRUSSEL, J.A.: *Casebook of a Crime Psychiatrist*, New York (1968)
BURRARD, Gerald: *The Identification of Firearms*, London (1951)
CAMERON, J.M. and SIMS, B.G.: *Forensic Dentistry*, London (1973)
CAMPS, Francis E.: *Camps on Crime*, Newton Abbot (1973)
CAMPS, Francis E. with BARBER, Richard: *The Investigation of Murder*, London (1966)
CAMPS, Francis E. (Ed): *Gradwohl's Legal Medicine*, Bristol (1976)
CANTER, David: *Criminal Shadows*, London (1994)
ERZINCLIOGLU, Z.: *Forensics*, London (2006)
EVANS, C.: *The Father of Forensics*, London (2009)
FATTEH, Abdullah: *Medico-Legal Investigation of Gunshot Wounds*, New York (1976)
FERLLINI, R.: *Silent Witness*, London (2007)
FIRTH, J.B.: *A Scientist Turns to Crime*, London (1960)
GARRET, J. and NOTT, A.: *Cause of Death*, London (2001)
GAUTE, J.H.H. and ODELL, R.: *Murder Whatdunit?*, London (1982)
GODDARD, Kenneth W.: *Crime Scene Investigation*, Reston (USA)
GOFF, M. Lee: *A Fly for the Prosecution*, Harvard University Press (2000)

GLAISTER, J.: *The Power of Poison*, London (1954)
GROSS, Hans: *Criminological Investigation*, London (1962)
HASTINGS, Macdonald: *The Other Mr. Churchill*, London (1963)
HELPERN, Milton: *Autopsy*, New York (1977)
JACKSON, Robert: *The Crime Doctors*, London (1966)
KIND, Stuart: *Science Against Crime*, London (1982)
KNIGHT, Bernard: *Murder, Suicide or Accident*, London (1971)
KOEHLER, S.A.: *Jumped, Fell or Pushed?*, London (2009)
KOLLER, Larry: *Guns*, New York (1974)
LANE, Brian: *Encyclopaedia of Forensic Science*, London (1992)
LEWIS, A.A.: *The Evidence Never Lies*, New York (1984)
LUCAS, A.: *Forensic Chemistry and Scientific Criminal Investigation*, London (1921)
LUCAS, N.: *The Laboratory Detectives*, New York (1971)
LUNDE, Donald T,: *Murder and Madness*, San Francisco (1976)
MACINNIS, P.: *Poisons*, New York (2004)
MAPLES, W.R.: *Dead Men Do Tell Tales*, London (1994)
MILLEN, Paul: *Crime Scene Investigation*, London (2010)
MILLER, Hugh: *Traces of Guilt*, London (1995)
MITCHELL, C. Ainsworth: *The Scientific Detective and Expert Witness*, Cambridge (1931)
MOORE, P.: *The Forensics Handbook*, London (2004)
NEUSTATTER, W.L.: *The Mind of the Murderer*, London (1957)
NOGUCHI, T.: *Physical Evidence*, New York (1990)
NOGUCHI, T.: *Unnatural Causes*, London (1988)
ODELL, Robin: *Medical Detectives*, Stroud (2013)
OUGHTON, F.: *Murder Investigation*, London (1971)
PENRY, Jacques: *Looking at Faces*, London (1971)
RAGLE, Larry: *Crime Scene*, New York (1995)
ROSE, Andrew: *Lethal Witness*, London (2007)
SAUNDERS, K.C.: *The Medical Detectives*, London (2001)
SCHENK, G.: *The Book of Poisons*, London (1956)
SIMPSON, Keith: *Police: The Investigation of Violence*, London (1978)
SIMPSON, Keith: *Forty Years of Murder*, London (1978)

BIBLIOGRAPHY

SIMPSON, Keith: *Forensic Medicine*, London (1969)
SMITH, Sydney: *Mostly Murder*, London (1959)
SMYTH, F.: *The Causes of Death*, London (1980)
THORWALD, Jurgen: *Crime and Science*, New York (1966)
THORWALD, Jurgen: *The Marks of Cain*, London (1965)
THORWALD, Jurgen: *Dead Men Tell Tales*, London (1966)
THORWALD, Jurgen: *Proof of Poison*, London (1966)
WALSH, D. and POOLE, A.: *A Dictionary of Criminology*, London (1983)
WALLS, H.J.: *Expert Witness*, London (1972)
WALLS, H.J.: *Forensic Science*, London (1974)
WECHT, C.H.: *Cause of Death*, New York (1994)
WECHT, C.H.: *Crime Scene Investigation*, London (2004)
WILLIAMS, J.: T*he Modern Sherlock Holmes*, London (1991)
WOLFGANG, Marvin E.: *Patterns in Criminal Homicide*, Pennsylvania (1958)

INDEX

ABO blood grouping, 14, 29–30, 104–5, 137
  dried bloodstains, 128, 138
  secretors and non-secretors, 143, 160
Acid Bath Murderer (John Haigh), 150, 161–2
aconitine, 166
age estimation, 13–14, 64
alkaloid poisoning, 161, 166, 167
Almodovar, Louisa, 73–4
Almodovar, Terry, 74–5, 116–17
American Academy of Forensic Sciences, 120–1
American Journal of Physical Anthropology, 129
Amoëdo, Oscar, 42, 89
anatomy, 12, 170–1
Anatomy of Violence, The: The Biological Roots of Crime (Raine), 84
ancestry estimation, 65
Anthropological Research Facility (ARF) *see* Body Farm
anthropology, forensic, 63–8
  early history, 129, 135
  facial modelling and reconstruction, 65, 115–16, 149–50
  historical deaths investigations, 66–7, 135, 146
  identifying skeletal remains, 63–4, 66, 67–8, 106–7, 138–9
  methods, 64–5, 155
  radiography, 18, 95
  research facilities, 60, 66, 91, 145–6
  war dead identification, 67, 135
anthropometry, 92–3, 114–15, 151–2, 158
Antistius, 11
Argentina, 115, 172–3
arsenic
  in hair, 15, 26–7, 66–7
  Lafarge case, 24, 147, 152–3
  Marsh test, 23–4, 146–7, 159
  Smethurst case, 18, 27–8, 167–8
  Madeleine Smith case, 103
asphyxial death, 95, 96, 166–7
Australia
  Dingo Baby trial, 99–100
  Graeme Thorne kidnapping and murder case (1960), 75–6
autopsy *see* post mortem examination
Autopsy (Helpern), 21, 126

ballistics, forensic, 35–40
  bullet wounds, 39–40, 174–5
  cartridges, 36
  case studies, 37–8, 39, 104, 118–19, 162, 173
  comparison microscopy, 19, 121–2
  evidence criteria, 38
  history, 19, 35
  instrumentation, 36, 121
  matching bullets to specific gun, 19, 35–6, 90–1
  microphotography, 35, 104, 121–2
  propellants and powder residues, 32, 122, 163

INDEX

rifling characteristics, 36, 174
  see also Burrard; Churchill; Goddard; Gravelle; Smith (Sir Sydney); Waite
Balthazard, Victor, 15, 26, 36, 90–1
Barr, Murray Llewellyn, 91
Barr body, 91
Bass, William, 59–60, 61, 66, 91
Bayle, Edmond, 92
Bazar de la Charité fire, 42, 89
Berger, Thomas, 131
Bergeret, Louis, 53–4, 119
Bertillon, Alphonse, 92–4, 115
Bertillonage, 92–3, 114–15, 126, 158
Bertram, Ewart George, 91
Biggar murder case (1967), 46–8
biometry, 154
bite marks, 45–50, 89, 162
Blazing Car Mystery (1930), 63–4
blood
  absorption test, 128
  antitoxins, 94
  and asphyxia, 166–7
  circulation, 145
  clotting, 44
  coagulation, 96
  composition, 91, 139
  DNA and, 130
  and drowning, 116
  precipitin test for, 14, 29, 94–5, 169–70
  presumptive tests for, 28–9
  rhesus antibodies, 104
  sex determination, 91
  typing, 14, 29–30, 104–5, 128, 137–8, 156
blood spatter analysis, 14, 132–3, 143–4
blowflies, 55–6, 57
bluebottles *see* blowflies
Bocarmé, Hippolyte de, 24, 165
Body Farm, 59–60, 66, 91
bombings
  Blitz, 43
  Mad Bomber of New York, 97
  Quebec Airways DC-3 (1949), 32–4
bones, 64–5
  see also skeletal remains
Bordet, Jules, 94–5
born criminal, 84, 141
botany, forensic, 69–79, 116–17
Bradley, Stephen Leslie, 76
brain imaging, 20, 84

Branch Davidians, 66
Brash, James Couper, 18, 95, 118
Brinkley, Richard, 30–1
Brittle, William, 57–8
Brouardel, Paul, 95–6, 126
Brown, Dr. Frederick Gordon, 18
Browne, Frederick Guy, 39, 104
Browne and Kennedy case (1927), 39, 104
Brussel, James, 96–8
Buchanan, Robert, 176
bullet tracks, 40
bullets, 19, 35–6, 38–9, 90–1
  see also ballistics, forensic
Bureau of Forensic Ballistics, 19, 36, 174
burn victims *see* fire victims
Burrard, Gerald, 98
Byrnes, Thomas, 98–9

cadaveric alkaloids, 161, 166, 167
Caesar, Julius, 11
Calabar bean, 103
Calcar, Jan Stephen van, 12, 171
Cameron, James, 50, 99–100
Camps, Francis, 45, 100–1, 121
Canter, David, 101–2
Cardiff missing person case (1989), 62, 110
Case of Oscar Slater, The (Doyle), 106
Casebook of a Crime Psychiatrist (Brussel), 97–8
Casper, Johann Ludwig, 102
casts, 156
Central Park, New York, 73–4, 116
Chamberlain, Lindy, 100
chemistry, forensic, 23–34, 142
Chisham, Colin, 174–5
Christie, John, 45, 123
Christison, Sir Robert, 102–3
Churchill, Robert, 38–9, 98, 103–4
Cocks, Detective Sergeant F.B., 76
comparison microscope, 19, 36, 37, 38, 118, 122
computer assisted tomography, 20
computers, applications to forensic science, 20
Coombs, Robin, 104–5
Copeland, Joseph J., 74–5
Coppolino, Carl, 125–6
coroner system (in USA), 19
Crafts, Richard, 138–9

INDEX

Cream, Thomas Neill, 83–4
Crick, Francis, 113
crime scene investigation (CSI)
   contact traces, 16, 72, 106
   development of scientific methods, 14, 17, 30, 138
   documenting, 17–18, 130, 159
   evidence collection, 20, 28
   preserving the scene, 17, 40, 112
   training, 62, 133–4
   see also blood spatter analysis; hair analysis; trace evidence
crime scene photography, 130, 159
Crimes Club, The, 106
Criminal Investigation (Gross), 24
criminal mapping, 102
criminal profiling, 96–8, 101–2, 109
criminal responsibility, 81–2, 150
Crippen, Dr. Hawley Harvey, 164
Cummings, Homer S., 37–8
cypress trees, 76

dactyloscopy, 126–7, 172–3
Dahma, Father Hubert, 37
Dahmer, Jeffrey, 67–8
d'Autrement, Roy, 72, 125
de la Pommerais, Edmond, 167
Dead Men Do Tell Tales (Maples), 50–1, 146
Dead Men Tell Tales (Thorwald), 13
Death's Acre (Bass), 61, 91
decomposition of the body, 55, 59–60, 62, 119–20, 166
dentistry, forensic *see* odontology, forensic
dentists, role in forensic investigations, 43–5
dermal nitrate test, 32
digitalis poisoning, 167
diminished responsibility, 82
Dingo Baby trial, 99–100
disaster victim identification, 64, 68
dissection of human cadavers, 12, 102, 170
DNA fingerprinting, 19–20, 109, 129–30, 146
DNA screening (Pitchfork case), 130
DNA structure, 113
Dobkin, Harry, 44
Dobkin, Rachel, 43–4
document examination, 30–2, 121, 148–9, 153, 168–9
documentation of crime scene, 17–18, 130, 159
Dorsey, George, 107
Doyle, Sir Arthur Conan, 23, 69, 105–6, 140
drowning, 116
drugs, detection by maggots, 62, 119–20
Drummond, Edward, 81
Duffy, John Francis, 101
Duncan, Andrew, the elder, 16, 107–8
Duncan, Andrew, the younger, 16
Durham Rule, 82
dust, 75, 78
Dwight, Thomas, 64, 106–7

E-FIT system, 148, 156
ears, and trace evidence, 78–9
Eber, Wilhelm, 108
Eckert, William, 108–9
Edalji, George, 105, 106
Elwell, Joseph Bowne, 151
Emmett-Dunne, Sergeant Frederick, 100–1
entomology, forensic, 53–62
   body farm research, 59–60, 66, 91
   Brittle case, 57–8
   Cardiff missing person case (1989), 62, 110
   Falls Church murder case (1984), 60–1
   history, 53–5, 119, 147–8
   Honolulu murder case (1996), 61–2
   life cycle of flies, 55–6, 57
   pig carcass research, 59
   Ruxton case, 55–6, 118
   time of death estimation, 54, 55–6, 57, 58, 61–2, 91, 147–8
   in USA, 58–9
   see also maggots
epigenetics, 85
Erzinclioglu, Zakaria, 62, 109–10
eugenics, 115
evidence collection, 20, 28
exchange of evidence principle, 14, 16, 25, 72, 140
expert testimony, 18, 175
Expert Witness (Walls), 175
explosives, 32–3
   see also bombings

INDEX

'Eye of Osiris, The' (Freeman), 42

facial identification systems, 148, 155–6, 171
facial modelling and reconstruction, 65, 115–16, 149–50
see also moulage
Falls Church murder case (1984), 60–1
Faulds, Henry, 110–12, 128
faunal succession, 55
Faurot, Joseph, 71, 112, 127
Federal Bureau of Investigation (FBI)
  ballistics department, 39, 119
  crime laboratory, 59
  Fingerprint Bureau, 112
  and flawed evidence, 15
  and forensic entomology, 59, 62
  and identification of skeletal remains, 135
  and serial murder, 151
  Waco siege shoot out, 66
Finger Prints (Galton), 115
fingernail scrapings, 25, 70, 77, 78, 140
fingerprinting
  in Argentina, 115, 172–3
  forged, 159
  in Germany, 108, 123–4
  history, 93–4, 110–12, 114–15, 127–8
  identification and classification, 110, 126–7, 145, 157
  latent prints, 108
  in USA, 71, 112
fir trees, 72, 124
fire scene investigation, 51–2, 63–4, 113
fire victims
  Bazar de la Charité fire, 42, 89
  Kuwaiti murder victim case (1993), 149–50
  Meek case, 51–2
  Rouse case, 63–4
  Tetzner case, 134
  Waco siege, 66
firearms *see* ballistics, forensic
Firth, James, 112–13
Fisher, John H., 36, 121
'Five Orange Pips, The' (Doyle), 69
flies, 55–6, 57
Fly For The Prosecution, A (Goff), 61, 120
footprint analysis, 163
Forensic Dentistry (Cameron and Sims), 50, 99
Forensic Dissection (Casper), 102
forensic examiners, qualities needed, 16
Forensic Medicine (Simpson), 162
Forensic Medicine and Toxicology (Smith), 162–3
Forensic Odontology (Gustafson), 48, 50, 123
forensic science, reputation of, 18, 167–8
Forensic Science (Walls), 28, 174
forensics: origin of term, 11
forged signatures, 152, 168–9
Forum Romanum, 11
Franklin, Rosalind, 113
Freeman, R. Austin, 42
Fry, Sir William Kelsey, 44
fungi, 75, 78
Furness, John, 46, 49–50, 52

Gall, Franz, 114
Galton, Sir Francis, 111, 114–15, 126–7
gender determination, 64, 91
genetic fingerprinting *see* DNA fingerprinting
Gerasimov, Mikhail, 115–16, 149
Gettler, Alexander O., 74, 116–17
Glaister, John, 18, 26, 55–6, 95, 117–18
Glasgow Dental Hospital, 46
Goddard, Calvin, 19, 36, 37, 39, 118–19, 174
Goff, M. Lee, 61–2, 119–20
Gonzales, Thomas, 120
Gorse Hall murder trial (1910), 29
Gouffé, Toussaint-Auggsent, 13–14, 136–7
Gourbin, Emile, 25, 140
Gradwohl, Rutherford, 101, 120–1
Grant, Julius, 121
grasses, 71, 74–5, 116–17
Gravelle, Philip, 19, 36, 118, 121–2, 174
Gross, Hans, 17, 24, 71, 122–3, 131
Guay, Albert, 33
guns *see* ballistics, forensic
gunshot wounds, 39–40, 174–5
Gustafson, Gösta, 48, 50, 99, 123
Gutteridge, PC George, 39
Guy, William, 17

Haigh, John (Acid Bath Murderer), 150, 161–2

INDEX

hair analysis, 15–16, 26–7, 66–7, 90, 117, 139
Hairs of Mammalia (Balthazard), 15, 90
handprints, 108
handwriting analysis, 31–2, 168–9
hanging, 95, 166
  simulated to disguise homicide, 96, 100–1
Harris, Carlyle, 176
Harvey, Warren, 46–8
Hastings, Macdonald: *The Other Mr Churchill*, 39, 104
Hauptmann, Bruno, 73, 135, 153, 169
Hay, Gordon, 46–8, 162
Heath, Neville, 150
Heindl, Robert, 123–4
Heinrich, Edward, 71–2, 124–5
helixometer, 36, 121
Helpern, Milton, 21, 109, 120, 125–6
Henry, Sir Edward, 94, 115, 126–7
Herschel, William, 110–11, 114, 127–8
Heslin, Father Patrick, 172
Hightower, William, 172
Hinckley, John, Jr., 83
histology, 17
historical deaths, investigating, 27, 66–7, 135, 146
Hitler's Diaries, 31–2, 121
Hogg, Quintin, QC, 53
Holmes, Sherlock, 23, 69, 105, 106, 142
Holzer, Franz, 128–9
Homicide Act (1957), 82
Honolulu murder case (1996), 61–2
Hoover, J. Edgar, 39, 59
Hrdlicka, Ales, 65, 129
Human Identification Laboratory, University of Florida, 50, 66, 145–6

Identification of Firearms, The (Gunther and Gunther), 38
Identification of Firearms and Forensic Ballistics, The (Burrard), 98
Identikit, 148, 155
ink testing, 30–1, 148–9
insanity, 81–2, 83
insect biology *see* entomology, forensic
Institute of Police Science, Lausanne, 159
International Reference Organisation in Forensic Medicine (INFORM), 109
investigative psychology, 101–2

iodine, fuming, 108, 125
IRA hitman bite mark case, 48–9
irresistible impulse, 82
Israel, Howard, 37–8

Jaccoud, Pierre, 170
Jack the Ripper murders, 18, 109
Japan, 110
Jeffreys, Sir Alec, 19–20, 129–30
Jennings, Paige, 51–2
Jeserich, Paul, 35, 130–1
Johnson, Karl, 49–50
Journal of Forensic Medicine and Pathology, 109

Keeler, Leonarde, 131–2
Keep, Nathan, 41
Kennedy, Robert F., 109
Kennedy, William, 39, 104
Kersta, Lawrence, 132
Killer Next Door, The (Norris), 152
Kirk, Paul, 132–3
Kockel, Richard, 35–6, 133–4
Koehler, Arthur, 72–3, 134–5
Kopkin, Barnet, 43–4
Koresh, David, 66
Krogman, Wilton, 135

La Faune des Cadavres (Mégnin), 54, 147
Laboratory for Plastic Reconstruction, USSR, 116
Lacassagne, Alexandre, 13–14, 19, 21, 35, 102, 136–7
Lafarge, Marie, 24, 147, 152–3
Lafelle, Marie, 25
Lamson, Dr. George, 161, 165–6
Landsteiner, Karl, 14, 29, 104, 137
Larson, John, 131, 172
L'Art Dentaire en Médecine Légale (Amoëdo), 42, 89
latent fingerprints, 110
Lattes, Leone, 137, 138
Laubach, Karl, 70, 157
Lee, Henry C., 138–9
Leeuwenhoek, Antonie *see* Van Leeuwenhoek, Antonie
Legal Medicine and Toxicology (Gonzales et al), 120, 126
lie detector, 131, 172
Lindbergh baby kidnapping (1932),

INDEX

72–3, 134–5, 153, 169
Locard, Edmond, 16, 25, 78, 136, 140–1
Lombroso, Cesare, 84, 141–2
Lucas, Alfred, 24–5, 142
Luetgert, Adolph, 107
Lynch, Gerald, 142–3

MacDonell, Herbert Leon, 14, 143–4
Macé, Gustave, 144–5
Mad Bomber of New York (George Metesky), 97
maggotology, 62, 110
maggots
  drug and toxin detection, 62, 119–20
  life cycle of flies, 55–6, 57
  maggotology, 62, 110
  spontaneous generation theory, 53
  trauma and wound impact, 60
Malik, Abdul (Michael X), 77
Malpighi, Marcello, 145
Manchester headless body case (1993), 65
Manual of Medical Jurisprudence (Taylor), 167, 168
Maples, William, 50–1, 66–7, 145–6
mapping, criminal, 102
Mars-Jones, Mr Justice, 50
Marsh, James, 23, 146–7
Marsh-Berzelius Process, 147
Marsh test, 23–4, 146–7
McDonald, Hugh, 148
McKenny-Hughes, Alfred, 53, 58
Mearns, Alexander, 55, 56
medicine, forensic, 11–21
Medicine, Science and the Law (journal), 101
Medico-Legal Aspects of the Ruxton Case (Brash and Glaister), 95, 118
Meek, Glyde, 51–2
Mégnin, Jean Pierre, 54–5, 147–8
Mengele, Josef, 109
Mens Rea (guilty mind), 81, 83
Metesky, George, 97
Michael X, 77
microphotography, 35, 104, 117, 121–2, 157
microscope, comparison, 19, 36, 37, 38, 118, 122
microscopy, 15, 17, 70, 121, 139–40, 157
  see also comparison microscope
microtome, 157

Milton Helpern International Center for the Forensic Sciences, 109
Mind of the Murderer, The (Neustatter), 82, 150
Mitchell, Charles Ainsworth, 31, 148–9
mites, 54
M'Naghten, Daniel, 81
M'Naghten Rules, 81–2
Modern Criminal Investigation (Söderman and O'Connell), 163
morphine poisoning, 176
mortuary working conditions, 102
moulage, 156
mould (fungus), 75
mug shots, 93, 99
Muncie, William, 46
mushroom grower murder case, 78–9
Mussolini's diaries, 121

Napoleon, 27
Nature (journal), 110, 111
Neave, Richard, 149–50
neurocriminology, 84–5
neurolaw, 84
Neustatter, W. Lindesay, 82, 150
New York Police Department (NYPD), 97, 98, 112, 163
New York Times, The, 83
Newsweek, 83
Nicholas II, Czar (and family), 135, 146
nicotine, 24, 165
Noguchi, Thomas, 109
Norris, Charles, 19, 120, 150–1
Norris, Joel, 151–2
Norway, 42–3

occupational marks on body, 123, 167
odontology, forensic, 41–52
  age estimation from teeth, 13–14, 64
  bite marks, 45–50, 89, 162
  dental practitioner role, 44–5
  early history, 13–14, 41–2
  identifying human remains, 42, 43–5, 50–2, 65, 67, 89, 123, 139
  marks in the mouth, 123
  publications, 42, 48, 50, 89, 99, 123
  in Scandinavia, 42–3
offender profiling, 96–8, 101–2, 109
Orfila, Mathieu, 17, 24, 147, 152–3, 165
Osborn, Albert Sherman, 153, 168
Ottolenghi, Salvatore, 154

INDEX

paint, 92, 174
Panicum dichoth milleflorium, 74–5, 116–17
paper, 30, 121
Paré, Ambroise, 154
Parker, Reginald, 31
Parkman, George, 41
Patrick, Albert, 168–9
Payne, Jerry, 59
Pearson, Karl, 64, 115, 154–5
Pearson's Formula (estimating stature), 155
pelvis, determining sex, 64
Penry, Jacques, 155–6
Pépin, Franchère, 33
Pereira, Margaret, 156
Photofit system, 148, 155–6
photography, forensic *see* crime scene photography; microphotography; mug shots; spectrophotometry; superimposed photographs; X-ray photography
phrenology, 114
physostigmine, 103
pig carcass research, 59
Pinus radiata, 79
Pitchfork, Colin, 130
Podmore, William, 149
poisoning cases
  Hippolyte de Bocarmé, 24, 165
  Richard Brinkley, 31
  Carl Coppolino, 125–6
  Thomas Neill Cream, 83
  Marie Lafarge, 24, 152–3
  George Lamson, 161, 165–6
  morphine poisoning, 176
  Napoleon, 27
  Edmond de la Pommerais, 167
  ptomaine poisoning, 161, 166, 167
  Margery Radford, 26–7
  Thomas Smethurst, 8, 27–8
  Madeleine Smith, 103
  Zachary Taylor, 27, 66–7
  see also arsenic; Marsh test; toxicology
police science, 17
pollen grains, 77–8
Poller, Alphonse, 156
polygraph, 131–2
Popp, Georg, 69–71, 156–7
portrait parlé (speaking likeness), 93, 148, 154
post mortem examination
  documenting, 18
  history, 12–13, 102
  mortuary working conditions, 102
  trace evidence collection, 16
  virtopsy, 20
postmortem interval *see* time of death
potential dangerousness, 152
powder residues, 32, 122, 163
precipitin test, 14, 29, 94–5, 169–70
prefrontal cortex, 84
Professional Criminals of America (Byrnes), 99
profiling, criminal, 96–8, 101–2, 109
prussic acid, 31
psychiatry, forensic, 81–5, 150, 151–2
ptomaine poisoning, 161, 166, 167
Purkinje, Johann Evangelista, 157–8

Quebec Airways DC-3 bombing (1949), 32–4
questioned documents *see* document examination
Quetelet, Lambert, 93, 158

racial origin estimation, 65
Radford, Margery, 27
radiography, 18, 95
Railway Rapist (John Duffy), 101
Raine, Adrian, 84
ransom note examination, 153
Ravachol, 93
Reagan, Ronald, 83
Redi, Francesco, 53
Regan, Donald, 83
Reiss, Rudolph, 158–9
rhesus antibodies, detection of, 104
Rice case (1902), 168–9
Rogerson, Mary, 56
rogues gallery, 99
Romanoffs (Russian royal family), 135, 146
Roughead, William, 106
Rouse, Alfred Arthur, 63–4
Ruest, Généreux, 33
Ruxton, Buck, 18, 55–6, 95, 117–18, 162

Sacco, Nicola, 19, 37, 118–19
Sacco and Vanzetti case (1927), 19, 37, 118–19

INDEX

saliva test, 138, 143, 160
Scheele, Karl, 23, 146, 159–60
Schiff, Fritz, 160
Scientist Turns to Crime, A (Firth), 113
Scotland Yard, 111, 115, 127
Scuola di Polizia Scientifica, Rome, 154
Selmi, Francesco, 161
semen, 138, 160
Serial Killers (Norris), 151–2
serial murder, 151–2
serology, 94–5, 104–5, 160
  see also blood; saliva test; semen
sex determination, 64, 91
Shaw, Eric, 63–4
Shaw, George Bernard, 104
Sheppard, Sam, 132–3
Siefert, Leonard, 70–1
signatures, disputed, 153, 168–9
Simpson, Keith, 161–2
  crime scene sketches, 18
  Rachel Dobkin case, 43–4
  foreword to *Forensic Dentistry*, 50
  John George Haigh case, 161–2
  Gordon Hay case, 47–8, 162
  Peter Thomas case, 57–8
  Tunbridge Wells bite mark case (1948), 45
  on Dr Hamish Walls, 174
Sims, Bernard, 50, 99
Siskiyou train robbery case (1923), 71–2, 124–5
skeletal remains
  differentiating human from animal, 65
  identifying, 63–4, 66, 67–8, 106–7, 138–9
Skerritt, Joe, 77
sketches of crime scene, 17–18
skull, and ancestry estimation, 65
Slater, Oscar, 106
Smethurst, Dr. Thomas, 18, 27–8, 167–8
Smith, Madeleine, 103
Smith, Sir Sydney, 16, 17, 18, 38, 162–3
Söderman, Harry, 163
soil analysis, 61–2, 70, 74, 157
soil disturbance, 77
Southampton Garage murder (1929), 149
Southport arson attack (1976), 49–50
spectrography, 74, 92, 163, 174
spectrophotometry, 31, 92

Spilsbury, Sir Bernard, 18, 63–4, 163–4
Stack, Sir Lee, 38, 162
Stas, Jean Servais, 24, 152, 164–5
Stas-Otto process, 164, 165
statistics, 158
stature estimation, 13, 64, 155
Stern (magazine), 31
Stevenson, Sir Thomas, 165–6, 175
Stielow, Charles E., 173
stigmata of criminality, 141
strangulation, 95, 96, 166
Structure of the Human Body, The (Vesalius), 12, 171
subungual debris, 25, 70, 77, 78, 140
succinylcholine chloride, 125–6
suffocation, 95, 96, 166
suicidal hanging, homicide disguised as, 96, 100–1
suicide, by shooting, 40
Sunday Times, The, 31
superimposed photographs, 48, 95, 117
Sûreté, 144, 171
System der Kriminalistik (Gross), 71, 123
Szibor, Richard, 78

Tardieu, Auguste, 95, 166–7
Tardieu spots, 166–7
tattoos, 136
Taylor, Alfred Swain, 18, 28, 167–8
  Principles and Practice of Medical Jurisprudence, 163, 166
Taylor, Zachary, 27, 66–7
teeth
  age estimation, 13–14, 64
  bite marks, 45–50, 89, 162
  human identification, 42, 43–5, 50–2, 65, 67, 89, 123, 139
Tetzner, Erich, 134
Texas bite mark case (1954), 45
Thomas, Peter, 57–8
Thorne, Graeme, 75–6
Thorwald, Jürgen, 13
time of death estimation
  body temperature, 136
  coagulation of blood, 96
  insect activity, 54, 55–6, 57, 58, 61–2, 91, 147–8
  lividity, 136
  plant evidence, 77
Times, The, 83

INDEX

tool mark analysis, 73
toxicology, 16–17, 23–4, 164–5
  see also arsenic; poisoning
toxins, detection by maggots, 62, 119–20
trace evidence
  autopsy collection, 16
  botanical, 71, 72, 74–6, 77–8
  dust, 75, 78
  in ears, 78–9
  evidential value, 106
  exchange principle, 14, 16, 25, 72, 140
  fibres and textiles, 131
  under fingernails, 25, 70, 77, 78, 140
  firearm powder residue, 32, 122
  hair, 15, 26, 66–7, 90, 117
  paint, 92, 174
  searching crime scene for, 20, 40
  soil, 61–2, 70, 74, 157
  wood chipping, 79
Traité des Poisons (Orfila), 152
Travia, Francesco, 151
Tunbridge Wells murder case (1948), 45
typescript examination, 153
tyre mark analysis, 163
Tyrrell, John F., 168–9

Uhlenhuth, Paul, 14, 29, 138, 169–70
Undritz, Erik, 170

Van Leeuwenhoek, Antonie, 139–40, 145
Vanzetti, Bartolomeo, 19, 37, 118–19

Vesalius, Andreas, 12, 170–1
Vidocq, Eugène François, 171
Vietnam War, 67
virtopsy, 20
voiceprint identification, 132
Voirbo, Pierre, 144–5
Vollmer, August, 131, 132, 172
Vucetich, Juan, 115, 172–3

Waco siege (1993), 66
Waite, Charles E., 19, 36, 121, 173–4
Walls, Hamish, 28, 79, 174–5
war dead identification, 67, 135
Watson, James, 113
Weber, Jeanne, 96
Webster, John White, 41–2
Wecht, Cyril, 68
Wilkins, Maurice, 113
Willcox, William, 29, 143, 175–6
Williams, John, 104
Witthaus, Rudolph, 176
wood chipping, 79
wood forensics, 72–3, 79, 134–5
wounds, gunshot, 39–40, 174–5

X-ray crystallography, 113
X-ray photography, 18, 40, 44, 51, 117

Yamakami, K., 160

Zacchia, Paolo, 176–7
Zeigler, Tommy, 143–4

www.ingramcontent.com/pod-product-compliance
Lightning Source LLC
Chambersburg PA
CBHW062215080426
42734CB00010B/1897